GRADING FOR MUSICAL EXCELLENCE

MAKING MUSIC AN ESSENTIAL PART OF YOUR GRADES

Also by Paul Kimpton (with Delwyn Harnisch)

Scale Your Way to Music Assessment

Also by Paul Kimpton and Ann Kaczkowski Kimpton

Adventures with Music Series

Starting Early

Dog Tags

Summer of Firsts

GRADING FOR MUSICAL EXCELLENCE

MAKING MUSIC AN ESSENTIAL PART OF YOUR GRADES

PAUL KIMPTON
AND ANN KIMPTON

THE PODIUM SERIES

GIA Publications, Inc.
Chicago

G-8409

GIA Publications, Inc.
7404 South Mason Avenue
Chicago, IL 60638
www.giamusic.com

Copyright © 2013 GIA Publications, Inc.
All rights reserved.

Printed in the United States of America.

ISBN: 978–1–57999–962-9

CONTENTS

PREFACE

"Knowledge is useless unless you can apply it."

—Unknown

"Those who cannot change their minds cannot change anything."

—George Bernard Shaw

AN EMERGING EPIPHANY

I have been a victim of poor grading and evaluation systems and practices throughout my formative years and during my band-conducting years. It wasn't until the music faculty at my high school sat down to write this book about grading for music educators that the realization came that I had been a victim. A victim is someone who is acted upon, usually adversely, by a force, agent, or a system. For me, that system was a grading practice that was random, inconsistent, and mysterious. Growing up, I never showed anyone my report card, and I remember students sharing theirs only if they received all A's or close to it. Grades were something that were handed to students as a result of some inexplicable process; it wasn't until years later, as a teacher, when it dawned on me that all the grades I had gotten were not based upon what I could do with the information I learned, but rather on the amount of information I could regurgitate or how much effort or participation the teacher thought I had put forth. Once I realized that grades didn't define who I intellectually, was did I start to think it wasn't the grade that mattered, but rather how well I could apply the information. This application was the real measure of what I had learned.

I wish all the teachers I have had could see what I have accomplished with what they taught me. That single thought made me realize probably all the students I have taught were the victims of my own ill-thought-out grading system. It was the same one I had functioned under, or possibly not functioned under my entire student life. It was the only system I had known and, as a result, it was the one I used with the students I taught. As a student at the University of Illinois, I had no classes that showed future music educators how to develop a grading system or how to write test questions. It wasn't until half way through my teaching career that I realized the system being used by most music teachers was the same one their own directors had used.

Such a practice reminds me of the old story of the newly married young woman being told by her mother-in-law that in order to cook a delicious ham, you must cut the end of the ham off. "Why?" she asked, as she watched her mother-in-law carefully place the ham in the roasting pan and gently carve off about an inch of meat. "Because we've always cut the end off. That step is the secret to a moist and tasty piece of meat." You know the rest of the story. The daughter-in-law didn't understand the connection between cutting the end of the ham off and how it made the meat juicy, so she finally asked great, great grandmother about the tradition. Nana's response was "because the pan that I used was too small. In order to get the ham in my pan, I had to cut the end off."

That story brings us to the point and is directly related to grading practices: why do we do things the way we do? Is it just because we've always done it in the past? What are the grades we give our students based upon? Is the grading system we use based upon how we've been graded in the past?

Perhaps it's time to stop cutting the end off of the ham. As you read each chapter on our journey to creating a student-centered, differentiated grading system, maybe you need to scrap the old system and just get a bigger pan.

Throughout this book, the term *skill* is used. We use this term broadly, but in the context of this book, we are focused on **musical** *skills* that we define as the *fundamental abilities a musician must possess in order to perform, appreciate, and create a piece of music at a higher level.* A list of *musical skills* may include, for example, the ability to perform or create musical rhythms, to produce a pitch in tune, and to read musical notation. Part of the process encouraged in this book is for the teacher and the department to determine the skills that are valued in their own music classroom. Thus, when the word *skill* is mentioned, we hope that readers will consider what abilities students need in order to play, sing, read, understand, and appreciate or create music independently or with an ensemble. Finally, *skills* are intended to encompass and promote all aspects that define a competent musician musically, intellectually, and emotionally.

Each chapter will have two distinct voices. The first is written from Paul Kimpton's viewpoint concerning the application of the basic concepts of grading to a music program. The second voice is Ann Kimpton's, an assistant principal at a large suburban high school who takes a broader view of grades and how solid grading practices affect the learning environment in an effort to create self-directed learners.

FOREWORD

by

Paul Kimpton

When I was putting the finishing touches on our recent music assessment book, *Scale Your Way to Music Assessment*, published by GIA, I had to make a critical decision: Should I add a chapter about grading or keep the focus of the book on music assessment. In the end, I decided to leave grading out of the initial assessment book because a single chapter would not have done the subject justice. I wanted to properly explain the journey I took to create a grading system that students, parents, and administrators embraced for one, common purpose: **To create self-directed musicians and performers.** If you have read *Scale Your Way to Music Assessment*, you will remember the phrase, Independent Musicians Creating Quality Performances, or IMCQP. Likewise, the focus of this book is about how to create a self-directed musician (IMCQP) and the grading system is the vehicle for communicating to the students, parents, and administration where students are on their paths toward musical independence.

The co-author of *Scale Your Way to Music Assessment*, Dr. Del Harnisch, is a professor and renowned educator, who instructs teachers how to develop curriculum and assessments. For this book, however, I wanted a co-author from, as teachers call them, the dark side: the school administration. Music educators especially need to hear from administrators about the bigger picture that constitutes their schools. Since education has been a daily topic in our home for thirty-six years, where else could I find someone with administrative experience who not only understands the current climate of grading, but also knows about music education and music teachers? Therefore, I welcome Ann Kimpton's participation in the creation of this book, who is an assistant principal in charge of curriculum and instruction at a large, suburban Chicago high school. You will read about her perspective grading in the classroom and the need for educators to reform grading practices to better fit the twenty-first century school.

I have taught in elementary and junior high schools, and rural and suburban high schools. I have been a music department chair, dealing with parents' and students' grade issues. I have been a parent of two children and have been on the other side of the music grading system, one that was subjective, punitive, and not about improving musical skills and knowledge. I believe Ann and I can help you to understand current grading trends and research while helping you to develop a music grading system that will provide your students and parents with valuable information for improving their children's musical skills. It is no longer good enough to give students one grade that does not communicate the level and quality of their musical abilities and understandings.

By the time you finish reading about our journey, I hope you will be able to take the information and adapt it to your school community. Each school community is different, but the goal for why we grade is the same for all: to help students reach their fullest potential as musicians and understand what they need to do to become an *Independent Musician Creating Quality Performances*. To have a grading system that does not accomplish this goal is an injustice to music education, students, parents, administrators, and your community. Come join Ann and me as you begin the journey of *Grading for Musical Excellence—Making Music an Essential Part of Your Grades*.

Acknowledgements

The world as we have created it is a process of our thinking.
It cannot be changed without changing our thinking.
—Albert Einstein

The above quote by Albert Einstein is a perfect way to begin to thank the people who have helped change my thinking about music education and my place in it. They challenged me to reflect on what I do, why I did it, who I am, and what I could become.

This book is the sum of my support group, just as a concert is the sum of the performers. Therefore, I want to give credit to the following people for their help and support along the way:

- to my parents who have passed away but live through the experiences they gave me;
- to the hundreds of teachers and administrators I have worked with, and specifically Dr. Joseph Dalpiaz, who helped mold me into the educator, writer, musician, and clinician I am today;
- to all my students for allowing me to help them reach their potential while they helped me reach mine;
- to my co-author of this book who is also the co-author of my life: To Ann for editing and rewriting our lives together for thirty-seven years;
- to Carroll Gonzo my editor at GIA Publications and his wise suggestions; and,
- last and most important, to Alec Harris at GIA Publications, Inc., who has seen the potential in these books and has provided support and encouragement over the years. And, kudos goes to his hard-working staff for their efforts in making available a variety of books containing relevant topics to music educators throughout the world.

A richer, fuller life through music…
—Paul Kimpton

I would like to add to Paul's list of mentors who have helped us during our journey in education:

- to my father, Henry Kaczkowski, who supported his family with his paper route during the depression and was able to earn a doctorate in education after WWII thanks to the financial support of the GI Bill;
- to my mother, MaryAlyce Hornby Kaczkowski, who, as with her father and mother, became an educator and nurtured her children to love learning;
- to the educators I have met along the way for their insights and wisdom.

—Ann Kimpton

How to Use This Book

The co-authors, along with the staff at GIA publications, have made every effort to provide music educators with a wealth of information and material for creating, understanding, and implementing a differentiated grading program in which music is the focus.

Support groups are important for music educators who often feel isolated. As you read this book, the message board at our Web site (www.mpae.net) allows you to post a question that will be answered by the authors in addition to giving other educators a chance to respond to your questions. Many schools are doing great things with grading, and you will find you are not alone. Our Web site also has a list of dates and times when you may call and talk to Paul or Ann Kimpton on the phone for further help. As you work through each chapter, please share your questions and experiences, because our community of learners and we may help you on your journey to creating a differentiated grading system.

Grading for Musical Excellence: Making Music an Essential Part of Your Grades is designed to be used in many different ways and targets four distinct communities: music education professors, K – 16 music educators, pre-service music educators, and school administrators.

Music Education Professors

Grading is an effective tool at the higher-education level to motivate and instruct students in solid grading practices. If colleges and universities use an established grading system with their students, major benefits can be realized. The music education students will witness firsthand how instructors use grading to help foster skills and give feedback. College music educators are going to train the next generation of music educators therefore, using a grading system that can be duplicated in their future classrooms must be a major goal. This book can also be used as a textbook in music methods classes. The chapters are specifically written to foster discussions and promote the design of a student-focused grading system that will be used from the first day of teaching forward. Other areas of use for *Grading for Musical Excellence* in a music education methods class may include how to:

- implement a grading program based upon best practice;
- change a toxic culture;
- write specific learning targets;
- teach students how to write specific goals;
- use data to adjust instruction;
- motivate students;
- use grades to provide feedback to students in areas of their strengths and weaknesses;

- use student feedback to improve instruction;
- create a culture of learning;
- manage time effectively; and
- develop student accountability.

K-16 MUSIC EDUCATORS

The second community involves current K-16 music educators, the front-line troops in the battle to save music education. These educators face ever-growing pressure to expand grading in the classroom that promotes and measures a student's intellectual, emotional, and musical growth. A music educator who implemented the grading system described and a secondary administrator who worked closely with music teachers wrote this book. Teachers will be able to apply the material directly to their own teaching and evaluation practices and begin to see the results in their students' skill development and musical growth. By following the steps set forth in this book, a district could adapt these ideas to their particular schools and communities without having to "start from scratch." Other uses of *Grading for Musical Excellence* in a K-16 setting may include how to:

- implement a grading program based upon best practice;
- change a toxic culture;
- write specific learning targets;
- teach students how to write specific goals;
- use data to adjust instruction;
- motivate students;
- use grades to provide feedback to students in their areas of strengths and weaknesses;
- use student feedback to improve instruction;
- create a culture of learning;
- manage time effectively; and
- develop student accountability.

PRE-SERVICE MUSIC EDUCATORS

The third community, the music educators of the future, is the most important group of all. Young educators who enter their field often have limited exposure to music programs in other schools. This narrow experience, time and again, results in first-year teachers trying to duplicate their high school or college experiences. *Grading for Musical Excellence* provides novice teachers with another model to consider when designing a total grading system. Young educators have a tough job indeed, repeatedly having ensembles perform just weeks after the opening of school. Furthermore, they must teach students how to improve individual musical skills. *Grading for Musical Excellence* will get them to improve quickly those skills through grading not as judgment but as feedback, thus creating a system that is applicable and supported by administrators. *Grading for Musical Excellence* for pre-service or novice teachers may include how to:

- implement a grading program based upon best practice;
- change a toxic culture;
- write specific learning targets;
- teach students how to write specific goals;
- use data to adjust instruction;
- motivate students;
- use grades to provide feedback to students in areas of their strengths and weaknesses;
- use student feedback to improve instruction;
- create a culture of learning;
- manage time effectively; and
- develop student accountability.

ADMINISTRATORS

The last community, administrators, is one that must not be neglected, since they hold the key to the future of music education in the schools. With diminishing budget resources and greater accountability to state and/or national standards and assessments, administrators face decisions about how to divvy up the funds. *Grading for Musical Excellence* will help music educators justify their programs as being an integral part of the curriculum, teaching crucial skills that may not be taught in any other discipline.

Developing a solid grading program based upon current best practices will also alleviate the conflicts that arise when students or parents challenge grades that seem to be inconsistent and/or unfair. This book will also allow administrators who have no previous experience in music to understand the components of a strong music program that is student centered and based upon encouraging students to develop musical skills. Other uses of *Grading for Musical Excellence* may include how your music faculty can:

- implement a grading program based upon best practice;
- change a toxic culture;
- write specific learning targets;
- teach students how to write specific goals;
- use data to adjust instruction;
- motivate students;
- use grades to provide feedback to students in areas of their strengths and weaknesses;
- use student feedback to improve instruction;

- create a culture of learning;
- manage time effectively;
- develop student accountability; and
- assist administrators in understanding the components of a well-rounded music education program.

CHAPTER 1
SETTING THE STAGE FOR CHANGE

In order to address these two questions, why do we grade and what is the purpose of grades, let's go back to 1986. This date was when, as a music department, we came to the realization that our way of dispensing grades as well as our music department's grading system were not improving instruction and learning in the classroom.

It was a Monday morning in January, two weeks after the semester grading period had ended, as I checked my mailbox before band. My first semester teaching at a large Chicago suburban high school had concluded, and my ninth year of teaching music. Along with the usual daily announcements and mail was a computerized breakdown of our department grades and a hand-written note from my principal, Dr. Joe Dalpiaz. If you knew Joe, you would have understood the power of this note. Joe had circled the percentage of "A" grades the music staff had given and the percentage of "As" given by each department in the rest of the school. Next to the circled percentages were three hand-written words.

Let's discuss this!

In those days, we didn't have e-mail, so people tended to talk face-to-face, which may be hard to believe nowadays. The door to Dr. Joe's office was open, so I stuck my head in and asked, "Before we meet, I want to get the staff's syllabi and the grading systems and tests they've been using. We can then discuss the print-out you gave me. We have a department meeting scheduled for Wednesday. What time's good for you to meet? "

Joe leaned back in his chair and put his hands behind his head. "Friday at 10 o'clock. Be sure to bring all of the music department's grading guidelines and syllabi." Leaving his office, I went to the copier and copied the sheets he had given me and added to the hand-written note.

Come prepared to discuss Dr. Joe's note at the department meeting this Wednesday. Please bring your grading guidelines and syllabi for the last semester.

I put the notes in the choir and orchestra directors' mailboxes and walked back to the band room for rehearsal. About half way down the hallway, I stopped "dead in my tracks" and realized the power of his note as a flood of questions rushed into my mind.

How could I justify giving ninety percent of the students an A?
What were the grades based upon?
What did the grades mean?

What musical skills, if any, were being measured?

How were these skills being measured?

These were just a few of the questions that rushed through my mind. I then realized that my staff would have the same reaction. Before you continue reading, take out your current grading system and your syllabi for the past year. Now answer the following questions based upon your department's current grading system.

PAUSE

GRADING QUESTIONS

Mentally answer "yes" or "no" to each of the following questions. Consider your reason(s) and the approximate weight given to participation and its relevance to the total grade.

1. What is the grade distribution of your classes?
2. Are your grades based solely upon performance evaluation from the podium?
3. Do your grades take into account participation?
4. Do your grades take into account attendance?
5. Do your grades take into account attitude?
6. Do your grades take into account individual improvement of musical skills?
7. Do your grades take into account attainment of specific musical skills?
8. Are written theory skills taken into account in your grades?
9. Are listening skills taken into account in your grades?
10. Are all students graded on the same criteria by all teachers in the department?
11. Could your students and their parents explain what musical skills are valued in your program?
12. Could you show students their growth on specific music skills?
13. Do you give a pretest each fall to determine individual performance skills, written theory skills, and listening skills?

Now back to the story. On Wednesday morning we meet, as a department, to address Joe's note. It should be noted that the choir director and myself were both new hires at the school and we each had nine years of experience "under our belts." I showed my grades first and then they showed me theirs. After a lengthy discussion, I asked the dreaded question: Can we justify why we give so many "A" grades that are not based upon clear, individual musical skill development? The choir director looked at me and back down at her grades and said honestly, "I can't. I think I'm trying to encourage students to stay in an elective course. I also don't want to hurt their GPA. Plus, I want to get the enrollment numbers up. I believe that if students don't get an "A" in choir, they'll drop out. I'm new here and want the program to grow. Giving a grade of "A" is a way to help my program grow."

I didn't answer right away, which is rare, but after digesting her answer, I had to agree that although my grading system looked good on paper, there was very little real substance behind the actual grade given and the student's individual musical skill development. We agreed that we had to fix our department's grading system.

That Friday "Dr. Joe" and I discussed the music department's grading data. I told the truth. "On paper our grading system looks fine, but in reality, we are not doing a good job of measuring musicals skills and musical growth. The grades we give don't really mean anything." I told him that we had decided to change and showed him the time line for reworking our grading system and how we would work with him to create a viable grading system that communicated accurately the musical skills and growth our department valued. Joe was speechless to hear me say that we thought we were not doing a good job and that our grading system was more of a reward than a communication of musical skills and musical growth.

He said, "I've worked with music teachers for twenty years who have given the grade of "A" out in very high numbers, but I've never had anyone ever say that they needed to change. The fact that you have reflected on the data and are taking steps to create a system based upon individual musical skill development is tremendous."

We talked about current research and possible sources to use before ending the meeting. I walked out of his office and started the journey of laying the groundwork for *Grading for Musical Excellence.*

WHY DO WE GRADE?

When sitting down to begin the overhaul of our grading system with the staff, we had to answer this question: Why do we grade? At first this four-word question seemed almost too simple to answer until we each began to discuss our reasons.

PAUSE

Before continuing to read, take a few minutes to write your answer below. When each member of your department has finished, share your answer and the rationale supporting them.

Why do we grade?

_____

_____

_____

_____

The discussion at our department meeting centered on the following issues.

1. The school requires teachers to give grades. True, but this answer doesn't address the underlying meaning of what is the grade that we are mandated to assign?

2. Teachers assign grades to show progress. True, but then we discussed at length progress in what areas? Were we measuring general overall progress or progress in specific areas? Did our grades show progress in tone, range, diction, theory, aural skills, attitude, attendance, concert music, memorization, or comprehension?

3. Why were we weighting non-music categories more than music skills? Were we teaching the value of appropriate attitude and attendance, or were we teaching musical skills? What did we want that grade to represent?

4. A definition we found in the literature of why teachers grade came from Baily and McTighe (1996, 120) "The primary purpose of grades is to communicate student achievement … to students, parents, school administrators, post secondary institutions, and employers." This definition opened a discussion about how to develop a system for giving one grade that reflected multiple skills that may be learned in a class.

This discussion about the purpose of grading was one of the best academic and pedagogical conversations we ever had as a music department. The choir director remarked, "I enjoyed this discussion because we were able to get rid of our personal baggage. Instead we focused on what the students' needs are." She added, "I also think this meeting was the first time that I could discuss my grading system critically without feeling threatened or admitting that I might not be doing the best I can for the students."

Remembering that moment takes me back to chapter I in *Scale Your Way to Music Assessment* called "Forget The Baggage." That chapter encourages teachers to rid themselves of issues that would hold them back when creating an assessment program. It is time for you and your staff to do the same in order to create a system of *Grading for Musical Excellence*.

Take some time now before moving on in the book and complete the "Forget the Baggage" exercises in chapter two. Do them individually and then as a staff. These exercises will set the ground rules for further uninhibited discussions about grading.

ADMINISTRATIVE PERSPECTIVE

Music courses are not the only courses in which grade issues appear. When I was a Literacy Department Chair, I too had a similar experience. I would receive phone calls from parents who wanted to know why their child was recommended for enrollment in a remedial reading class when they had received an A in reading the year before. I had a difficult time explaining the rationale for that recommendation, especially when the student had received an A, which, in our system, indicated excellence. The student still required reading support, but our grades had been based more upon compliance and attitude than on actual communication of the student's skill level in reading. The teachers in the department, too, were fearful that if they actually graded based upon student skill level, students who were reading below level would be punished for their lack of reading skills. So, the dilemma was, how could teachers accurately communicate a student's progress in a subject matter? Thus, we had to throw out our old system of grading and begin anew.

Administrators see individual teachers whose grading practices are unfair and inconsistent. And, the more unfair and inconsistent, the more defensive the teacher becomes when questioned about a grade. That circumstance is why it is so important to complete the "Forget the Baggage" activity. A change in one's practice involves a change in one's belief system, and that change can only occur through honest reflection and forgetting your own personal grading baggage.

CHAPTER 2
FORGET THE BAGGAGE

The time has come to lay that baggage down and leave behind all the struggling and striving. You can be set free as you journey forward into a balance, healthy, and rewarding future.

—Sue Augustine

When traveling around the country giving workshops on assessment and grading, this author often encounters teachers, departments, and administrators who hold many pre-conceived ideas and/or negative opinions that make it impossible to move ahead in a discussion about grades. Their views were rooted in years of experiences that had negatively influenced their teaching. These experiences can also cause them not to look at ideas objectively. So, let's get rid of the baggage to begin our grading transformation journey. Illustration 1 provides an example of some of the reasons why music teachers may be reluctant to change their approaches to grading. Consider them before you make your own list of reasons that may prevent you from changing your current grading system.

"If I don't give all A's, students will drop out!"

"I've always graded on attitude and attendance."

"My administration wants my music classes to be a relaxing time for the students and a break in the day, but now it wants me to grade on growth?"

"Of course I can assess all of my students from the podium. I have no problem assigning grades based uoon my assessment of the students in rehearsal."

"I don't have time to hear students individually!"

"I used practice sheets when I grew up and so will my students!"

"How do you assign a grade to an aesthetic experience?"

ILLUSTRATION 1

COMMON GRADING BAGGAGE

Baggage will surface as you begin, as a department, to discuss the nature and purpose of grading and grades. Use the guidelines below as your "Robert's Rules of Order" for grading discussions.

- Don't let your personal past experiences get in the way of department discussions.
- Keep the focus on how to communicate to our musicians regarding where they are in musical skill and growth and comprehension development.
- Brainstorm: time is not a problem if you see the bigger picture and are organized.
- Avoid talking about what you think, but rather about what student musicians need. Don't get into an elementary versus general music versus instrumental versus vocal argument. Keep the focus on music skills.

Here are three areas to help focus your thoughts on the grading baggage exercises, which are presented in greater detail in chapter 5 in how Student Musical Understanding and Student Performance Skills are used to create Independent Musicians Creating Quality Performances. The Areas of Focus for grading shown in Illustration 2, which is a visual representation of how to keep the focus of your grades on music. The top two ovals, Student Musical Understanding and Student Performance Skills are the main areas where musical skills are taught. The bottom oval, Independent Musician Creating Quality Performances, is what can be accomplished by focusing on the top two ovals.

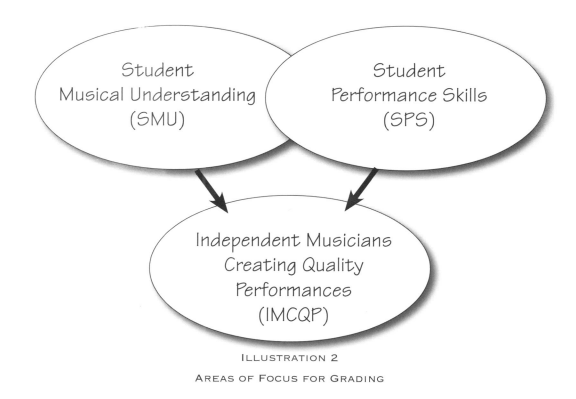

ILLUSTRATION 2

AREAS OF FOCUS FOR GRADING

TAKING NEGATIVE IDEAS AND CREATING POSITIVE EXPERIENCES

One of the author's best educational experiences occurred when enrolled in classes leading to a guidance and counseling certification. During counseling sessions, the professor would ask the students to write about their feelings and to look at problems in a variety of ways. The physical and mental process of putting feelings or thoughts on paper increases awareness of negative feelings. Taking a negative feeling and restating it in a positive way allows individuals to deal with negative issues and move ahead, thus not letting the issue inhibit their beliefs and emotions. Students who are able to see options to negative influences in their lives made the most progress. Appling this strategy to the author's own work and music staff discussions about developing a grading and music assessment program, our music staff found there were negative issues about grading that resolution seemed in order to move ahead as individuals and as a department.

In the next several pages you will write about your feelings and thoughts about grading so that any negative feelings that are articulated by your music staff can be discussed and resolved to avoid inhibiting your efforts toward developing a grading program.

No human being will work hard at anything unless they believe that they are working for competence.

—**William Glasser**

ADMINISTRATIVE PERSPECTIVE

One "squeaky wheel" can derail an entire meeting. Discussions go off topic when educators who resist change challenge an idea because they don't have proof that it works. Certainly, doing something differently just for the sake of change isn't a good practice, but keeping a system that is clearly broken is wrong. When department members resist letting go of personal baggage, their overt or even passive resistance can be a powerful force for a department to overcome. But, overcoming this resistance is an absolutely necessary step if a department is going to commit toward changing its grading philosophy.

It comes down to looking at grading through the lens of what is in the student's best educational and musical interest. Will changing your ideas of grading benefit the students' academic and musical growth? If you admit that it will, even though the change is difficult, it is a change that has to happen.

BAGGAGE EXERCISE – PART 1

Photocopy the next few pages. Gather all the teachers in your music department. On the lines below, ask each teacher to make an individual list of negative feelings or reasons for not wanting to change their grading system.

1. _____
2. _____
3. _____
4. _____
5. _____
6. _____
7. _____
8. _____
9. _____
10. _____
11. _____
12. _____
13. _____
14. _____
15. _____

BAGGAGE EXERCISE – PART 2

Have everyone read their lists aloud and explain why they wrote each reason. Remember to just listen with an open mind and not interrupt. Once all have shared their lists, integrate all the comments into one list so they can easily be referred to later.

1. _____
2. _____
3. _____
4. _____
5. _____
6. _____
7. _____
8. _____
9. _____
10. _____
11. _____
12. _____
13. _____
14. _____
15. _____
16. _____
17. _____
18. _____
19. _____
20. _____

BAGGAGE EXERCISE – PART 3

Now write the reasons **for** creating a grading system that is focused on musical achievement and not non achievement.

A key concept from *Scale Your Way to Music Assessment* is, "Creating a grading system for communicating to our parents, students, and administrators will help focus our teachers and students on improving musical skills through a clear understanding of where they are and what needs to be done to become Independent Musicians Creating Quality Performances."

_____

_____

_____

_____

_____

_____

_____

_____

_____

_____

_____

_____

_____

_____

BAGGAGE EXERCISE – PART 4

The next time you get together, have everyone read their reasons for creating a new grading system and record each reason. Select the positive statements that reflect your department's philosophy and put them in one document. This document will be your guide, along with the complete list of baggage that you will not bring to the table, to consult during your future discussions and work.

CHAPTER 3
ASSESSING YOUR CURRENT GRADING SYSTEM

The next step was the hardest for my department and will most likely be difficult for yours. Assessing your current grading system openly and critically is vital in order to separate *What is on paper* verses *What do I really do*. In the research we read as a faculty, we saw two reoccurring classifications of grading or assessment criteria: achievement and non-achievement.

Achievement activities would be considered performance or opportunities to demonstrate skills or knowledge, while non-achievement activities include attendance, attitude, time spent on practice, participation, effort, leadership, daily rehearsals and anything else that is not performance or knowledge-based.

Have your music faculty bring their current grading system and grade distributions for the past year and complete the grade analysis and grade categories worksheets presented below. Feel free to duplicate these pages as often as needed.

GRADE DISTRIBUTIONS

Your school may generate a grade distribution that will speed up the process. For each class you teach, complete the worksheet below. For example, you might have Concert Band, Wind Ensemble, Beginning Piano, AP Music Theory, and Freshmen Band. By examining single courses first, followed by grouping similar classes i.e., performance-based such as band, choir, and orchestra], and (non-performance based such as composition, AP Music Theory, or music appreciation) you will be able to compare individual teacher results to the overall department results.

Grade Distribution Worksheet

Class name_____Instructor_____

1st Quarter #A's____%_____ #B's____%_____ #C's____%_____ #D's____% #F's____%

2nd Quarter #A's____%_____ #B's____%_____ #C's____%_____ #D's____% #F's____%

Final Exam 1 #A's____%_____ #B's____%_____ #C's____%_____ #D's____% #F's____%

Semester 1 #A's____%_____ #B's____%_____ #C's____%_____ #D's____% #F's____%

3rd Quarter #A's____%_____ #B's____%_____ #C's____%_____ #D's____% #F's____%

4th Quarter #A's____%_____ #B's____%_____ #C's____%_____ #D's____% #F's____%

Final Exam 2 #A's____%_____ #B's____%_____ #C's____%_____ #D's____% #F's____%

Semester 2 #A's____%_____ #B's____%_____ #C's____%_____ #D's____% #F's____%

Or, you may want to analyze only the semester results.

Semester 1 #A's____%_____ #B's____%_____ #C's____%_____ #D's____% #F's____%

Semester 2 #A's____%_____ #B's____%_____ #C's____%_____ #D's____% #F's____%

GRADE CATEGORIES

Write each of your current grade categories in either the **Achievement Column** or the **Non-Achievement Column** and write the **weight/percentage** given to each category. Do this recording for each class you teach. For example, you might teach Concert Band, Wind Ensemble, Beginning Piano, AP Music Theory, and Freshmen Band. Remember, anything that is included as part of your grades should be included in one of the two columns. Feel free to duplicate this page as often as needed.

Grade Categories Worksheet

Class _____ Instructor_____

Achievement Task Performance, Skills, and Knowledge	Weight or Percent of Grade	Non-Achievement Tasks Attendance, Attitude, Practice, Participation, Effort, Leadership, and Daily Rehearsals	Weight or Percent of Grade

ANALYZING THE RESULTS

Now that you have finished examining the grade distribution and the category weights, what did you find? Answer the following questions by yourself and then follow-up with a departmental discussion.

What have you learned about the number and percentage of grades in your individual classes?

_____

_____

_____

_____

What have you learned about the number and percentage of grades in your department? Do your individual grades vary significantly from the overall music department's grades? If so, explain.

_____

_____

_____

_____

What have you learned about the balance between grades in the achievement category versus the non-achievement category?

_____

_____

_____

Based upon this analysis of your current grading system, what actual skills, academic achievement , and musical growth are valued in your classes and in your department?

_____

_____

_____

_____

Would your students and their parents be able to tell from their grades what musical skills are valued in this class?

_____

_____

_____

_____

Are your grades a mathematical average of all your assignments?

_____

_____

_____

_____

From your grades, is a student able to understand which skills are strengths and which are weaknesses?

_____

_____

_____

_____

By answering and discussing the previous questions as a music department, it is hoped that you discovered, as we did, that it is very important to look at all teachers' grades in relationship to the whole or the music department. Grading should be consistent in all music classes and the department. One can often hear students and parents comparing grades and expectations when discussing teachers and classes. Comments abound such as, "She would have gotten an A, if she had Mr. Jones," or "I can't believe I got Mrs. Johnson—she's so tough!" Inconsistency within a department creates the perception that grades are bestowed upon students based upon the prerogative of the teacher rather than providing feedback about student academic and musical achievement and/or growth in a course.

Additionally, these questions should have sparked discussion about what skills and knowledge are valued in your music department. Are your grades a reflection of musical skills or are they rooted in factors that are not explicit outcomes of the course?

WHAT DO WE WANT OUR GRADING SYSTEM TO LOOK LIKE?

What helped our music department get through this discussion was to think about how we wanted ourselves to be evaluated. We did so by answering the following questions. (The first few questions are related directly to the individual teacher and then the questions come back to their current grading system.) If you have completed the baggage exercise, then you will have an open discussion that will lead you to come together regarding how to grade as a music department faculty.

Write your answers separately, and then share them with each other. Once you have discussed questions 1 through 4, go to the last question (5) and write down what you have discovered about your current grading system.

1. Should administrators evaluate all teachers on the same skills and knowledge? Should those skills and knowledge be apparent to faculty members before they are evaluated? Should the standards to which teachers are held be the same regardless of who is doing the evaluation?

_____

_____

_____

_____

2. Have you or your child ever been the victim of unfair grading practices in a class? Explain. If you answered yes, how did you feel?

_____

_____

_____

_____

3. Should our students, parents, and administrators expect consistent levels of expectations and grading policies in our music department in all classes? Why or why not?

_____

_____

_____

_____

4. What are the benefits of consistent levels of expectations and grading? List them.

A._____

B._____

C._____

D._____

5. What positive and negative elements did you discover about your current system?

Negative	Positive
A._____	A._____
B._____	B._____
C._____	C._____
D._____	D._____
E._____	E._____
F._____	F._____

Here is what we found. When we finished analyzing our grades and answering the previous questions, we realized that the inconstancies in our grading and our level of expectations were because our current grading and assessment practices were not based upon clear learning targets that had explicit levels of expectation. We were shocked to have to admit that. Was it easy as a music faculty to admit we could do a better job? No, but we had a choice: Either ignore the problem or fix it. We fixed it in both our assessment program that we documented in the book *Scale Your Way to Music Assessment* and in this book, *Grading for Musical Excellence*. If you have read this book thus far, congratulations on being able to look honestly at your current system. Notice as you work through the book, the word *music* keeps coming to the forefront of your discussion. Perhaps you have begun to realize that what you are really trying to do each day is to communicate to your students where they are in becoming **Independent Musicians Creating Quality Performances.**

ADMINISTRATIVE PERSPECTIVE

When grading systems are murky, administrators are bombarded by requests from parents or students to avoid a certain teacher or to be enrolled in a course with a favored one. Likewise, we hear our share of complaints about teachers, and usually those complaints stem from a murky grading system and, by extension, grades students receive. Being the mediator in a battle between parents, teachers, and students over grades is not beneficial to anyone involved.

Students aren't looking for the easy teacher. However, students do deserve a teacher whose expectations are clearly defined and whose learning activities and assessments are linked to the specific skills and knowledge to be learned in the course. Students need the feedback grades can provide so they are able to reach a high level of musical competency by the end of the course.

Grades today are high stakes, and at the high school level, they may impact a student's grade point average, opportunities for college entrance, and scholarships. Therefore, teachers must be able to justify a grade and ensure that students have every opportunity to demonstrate competency. As the nation moves toward teacher evaluation that is linked to student performance, it becomes even more critical than ever to ensure that grades provide the feedback that will allow students to reach their highest level of competency.

CHAPTER 4
WHAT DOES THE RESEARCH TELL US ABOUT GRADING?
TAKING THE THEORETICAL AND APPLYING IT

When our department first looked for specific research about grading in the music classroom, we found it to be limited when compared to the amount of research about the non-music classroom. Numerous research studies and books exist that deal with general grading practices; however, the lack of music-focused grade research was troubling. Therefore, the belief emerged that we should employ the extensive research about other classroom grading practices and apply them to transform our music-grading procedures. The books listed at the end of this chapter are well worth the investment of your time:

After reading the research, we decided to tackle the following areas. Each area will be discussed further throughout the book. Non-musical achievement tasks should not affect a student's grade. At the very least, their inclusion should have only a small weight in the total grade. These tasks might include attendance, daily rehearsals, punctuality, in-class participation, responsibility, effort, citizenship, instrument care, leadership, and practice—in other words, anything that does not speak specifically to the development and comprehension of musical skills (see chapter 11).

Accordingly we would:
1. Adopt a skills-based grading system on the music skills we valued and wanted our students to master (see chapter 5);

2. Develop clear learning targets in two areas (see chapter 5);
   A. **Student Musical Understanding** (SMU), which consists of listening (aural), music theory, music terms or vocabulary, and genres.
   B. **Student Performance Skills** (SPS) which consist of skill demonstration through playing or singing.

3. Adopt, as a department, a *no zero policy* concerning assignments. We found the literature overwhelmingly was against giving a zero for missed or incomplete assignments. The mathematical hole created in a student grade with a zero offers students no chance to ever improve their grade (see chapter 7);

4. Create multiple opportunities for students to demonstrate musical skill development outside the rehearsal. Our only formative assessments of a student's musical growth would not be done from the podium during rehearsal in a large group setting (see chapter 9);

5. Develop a way to communicate to the students, parents, and administrators the students' progress on musical skill development more than once a quarter in a non-grade format. Grades to communicate skill level would be ongoing (see chapter 8);

6. Create numerous opportunities for students to demonstrate musical skills to outside evaluators to either validate the skill level or confirm the lack of musical proficiency (see chapter 9);

7. Develop a system of differentiated grading so we could challenge and support lower skilled and higher skilled students at the same time (see chapter 9);

8. Teach students how to self-assess and peer-assess musical skills (see chapter 8);

9. Involve students and parents in the process so that everyone understands the purpose of grades (see chapter 12);

ADMINISTRATIVE PERSPECTIVE

Why reinvent the wheel? The research exists, so why not use it to inform your classroom grading practices? We have had the privilege to work with Ken O'Connor who helped us tweak our grading practices so that it addressed our school's particular needs. The best advice is to read widely about best practices in grading and adapt those practices to fit your department's needs. Another word of advice is to avoid doing nothing because you want your grading policy to be perfect. Accept your efforts as a *work in progress* mentality and realize that doing something is better than adhering to a practice that is out of sync with the underlying principles of current research about grading.

Too often music departments lag behind the rest of a school in educational best practices. Why can't music teachers be the educational leaders in a school? Ask your administration to be included in staff development opportunities regarding assessment and grading. Then, after applying solid assessment and grading practices in your classes, share your expertise with the rest of the staff. Your "street credentials" will increase exponentially with staff and administration, as will the value of your program in relationship to the school community as a whole.

RECOMMEND BOOKS

Deci, Edward L. and Richard Flaste. (1996). *Why We Do What We Do: Understanding Self-Motivation.*

Guskey, Thomas R. (2008). *Practical Solutions for Serious Problems in Standards-Based Grading.* Thousand Oaks, CA: Corwin Press,

Robert Linn, Robert and David Miller. (2004). *Measurement & Assessment in Teaching.* Upper Saddle River, NJ: Prentice Hall.

Maehr, Martin and Larry Brakamp. (1986). *The Motivation Factor: A Theory of Personal Investment.* NY, NY: Lexington Books.

Marzano, Robert.(2000). *Transforming Classroom Grading.* Alexandria, VA: ASCD.

Marzano, Robert.(2006). *Classroom Assessment and Grading That Works.* Alexandria, VA: ASCD.

O'Connor, Ken.(2009). *How To Grade for Learning: Linking Grades to Standards.* Thousand Oaks, CA: Corwin Press.

Popham, James. (2010). *Classroom Assessment: What Teachers Need to Know.* Upper Saddle River, NJ: Pearson.

Stiggins, Richard J. (2000). *Student-Involved Classroom Assessment.* Upper Saddle River, NJ: Prentice Hall.

Stiggins, Richard J., Judy A. Arter, Jan Chappuis, and Stephen Chappuis. (2009).

Classroom Assessment for Student Learning: Doing it Rright—Using it Well. Portland, OR: ETS.

Tomlinson, Carol. (2008). *The Differentiated School: Making Rrevolutionary Changes in Teaching and Learning.* Alexandria, VA: ASCD.

Wormeli, Rick. (2006). *Fair Isn't Always Equal: Assessing and Grading in the Differentiated Classroom.* Portland, ME: Stenhouse Publishers.

CHAPTER 5
GRADING AND ASSESSMENT PRACTICES CANNOT BE SEPARATED

The purpose of assessment is to measure a student's knowledge and/or skills, and as a result, change one's instruction. In schools, we use grades to communicate that measurement to students, parents, and other educators. When you give a student a letter grade or percentage, you are inherently putting a value on the student's achievement in your class. In reality, assessment and grading are so closely intertwined that one cannot be discussed without the other.

HOW TO COMBINE THE TWO

The first issue we had to resolve was how to communicate to our students and parents that our grades were the culmination of numerous formative [informal] and summative [formal] assessments that were designed to show where their child's performance and theory skills were at the end of each quarter. Additionally, we decided to have students and classes set goals for musical achievement each quarter. With the teacher's assistance, each student would quarterly decide what specific musical skills would be the focus. The teacher would also set specific class goals that all students were going to work on together during each quarter and semester. To accomplish this ambitious move, we created a goal sheet for each quarter and a weekly goal and review sheet. In the book *Scale Your Way to Music Assessment* (pages 105, 106, and 107), you can read the entire story about how we created them. On the next few pages, I will discuss how these three sheets can be used in the classroom to create teacher and student ownership for learning. First let's look at the short- and long-term goals sheet below.

Our music department realized years ago that we were not clearly informing our students regarding our expectations each quarter or semester. In determining how to provide students with this information, it became necessary to clearly identify the learning targets for the day's rehearsal or class. Therefore, beginning each rehearsal by writing on the board the learning target(s) and students' role for the rehearsal, it helped the students achieve those targets. At the end of rehearsal, informal assessments helped to determine where the students were in reaching that day's goals and thus adjust instruction for the next day.

Now, take a minute to answer the following questions.

Do your students know the learning targets for each rehearsal and how they link to the goals for the course?

_____

_____

Do you assess students informally at the end of rehearsal to see if they have learned what you taught?

_____

_____

Do you provide students with feedback toward their learning goals and explain what needs to be done next?

_____

_____

Do your students know the course's goals and expectations for the quarter, semester, and year?

_____

_____

The following scenario demonstrates the importance of providing clear learning targets when grading students.

You are asked by your administration to attend a wilderness backpack team building camp with other department chairs to build a cohesive group. If you were going on this back-pack trip, would you want the guide to tell you where you were going and what you were going to accomplish? Would you want to know the physical requirements before you went? Each day would you want to know what was expected of you such as how many miles you would be hiking or if you would be climbing hills or crossing creeks? Would you want to know the approximate time to achieve the goal? At the end of the day, would you want the guide to assess your progress and provide specific feedback so you could reach the final destination? Would you want to have a clear understanding of the level of expectation and how you would be judged or evaluated on whether you met that level?

OR

Would you rather have no idea how far you would have to hike or what activities you were going to do? Would you rather just blindly follow the path? At the end of the day, you would have no idea what the next day was going to bring and how you were expected to interact with the group. Finally, at the end of the trip, the guide would give you a grade, but you didn't know what you were being graded on or at what point you were being assessed during the trip. When he gave you a grade of C (average) for your trip and efforts, you asked, "Why?" He responded that he didn't like your attitude, leadership skills, and he thought you made too many sarcastic comments and rolled your eyes. He felt you didn't give 100 percent of your effort and attention during the trip. And, by the way, he was sending a copy of your grade and the comments above to your administration.

Unfortunately, the second scenario could describe a typical student experience in a performance class. Do your students understand where they are going and what their role is in achieving that daily or quarterly goal? If you don't communicate frequently where students are going, how are they going to know whether they have reached the target?

WRITING DIRECTOR-ORIENTED GOALS

The intent here is to model the behavior of how to create short- and long-term goals for each class one teaches. It is essential for the students to see how goal setting is done and how to work toward achieving a long-term goal by setting short-term checkpoints or goals. Let's look at a sample goal sheet in Illustration 3 and observe how we would provide feedback to the students. The first goal sheet shown in Illustration 3 is blank and the second goal sheet represented in Illustration 4 has been completed with both director and student goals. This is a sample of one of the author's actual goal sheet and a sample actual student goal sheet.

ILLUSTRATION 3

GOAL SHEET

GOAL SHEET

Director Goals: Listed below are _____(Director Name)_____short- and long-term learning goals for the _____(Performing Group)_____ for the third quarter. By writing these goals, I am making a commitment to follow through.

Short-term goal 1:

Short-term goal 2:

Short-term goal 3:

Long-term goal 1:

Long-term goal 2:

Long term goal 3:

Student Goals: Now it is your turn. What are several short- or long-term goals you would like to work on this quarter based upon the data from your performances and first semester listening and written theory final? Be as specific as you can and be sure to follow through.

1. General Goal

2. Music Skill Goal

3. Music Skill Goal

4. Theory Goal

5. Listening Goal

ILLUSTRATION 4

GOAL SHEET

GOAL SHEET

Director Goals: Listed below are Mr. Kimpton's short- and long-term learning goals for the Symphonic Band for the third quarter. By writing these goals, I am making a commitment to follow through.

Short-term goal 1: Select ensemble members and music by January 30. All ensemble/solo events will be sent to the Illinois High School Association on January 31.

Short-term goal 2: Assign solos to accompanist by February 10.

Short-term goal 3: Select music for Spring Concert by March 10.

———————————————

Long-term goal 1: Students will learn band music by April 13. Each student will be assessed individually.

Long-term goal 2: Work with individual students in band to improve the ability to count and sing rhythms. This goal is based upon data from contest and juries.

Long-term goal 3: Work with individual students in band to improve ability to sight-read and use the Four-Point Plan of: Key, Time, How loud, How fast. Goal is based upon data from juries.

Student Goals: Now it is your turn. What are several short- or long-term goals you would like to work on this quarter based upon the data from your performances and first semester listening and written theory final? Be as specific as you can and be sure to follow through.

1. General- Turn in all paper work on time and work on writing a better weekly planning sheet. Reflect every other day on weekly progress.

2. Music skill- Learn the chromatic scale from Low G below the staff to high G above the staff, using all alternate fingering and maintaining the same tone quality throughout the scale.

3. Music skill- Practice sight-reading out of the sight-reading study book three times a week performing two, six-bar phrases focusing on key, time, how loud, and how fast.

4. Theory Goal- Learn to recognize intervals on paper from a minor 2nd to a major 7th taking two quizzes a week on the computer with ninety-percent accuracy.

5. Listening Goal- Learn to identify all major and perfect intervals on listening quizzes on the computer once a week with ninety-five percent accuracy.

Now let's look at the director goals found in Illustration 5 in more detail. Notice, the point here is to demonstrate goal writing for the students by providing short-term and long-term goals.

ILLUSTRATION 5

DIRECTOR GOALS

Director Goals: Listed below are Mr. Kimpton's short- and long-term learning goals for the Symphonic Band the third quarter. By writing these goals, the intention is to make a commitment to following through.

1. Short-term goal: Select ensemble members and music by January 30. All ensemble/solo events will be sent to the Illinois High School Association on January 31.
2. Short-term goal: Assign solos to accompanist by February 10.
3. Short-term goal: Select music for Spring Concert by March 10.
4. Long-term goal: Band music learned by April 13. Assess each student individually.
5. Long-term goal: Work with individual students in band to improve ability to count and sing rhythms. Goal is based upon data from contest and juries.
6. Long term goal: Work with individual students in band to improve ability to sight-read and use the Four-Point Plan of: Key, Time, How loud, and How fast. This goal is based upon data from the juries.

The teacher would hand this sheet out and explain the six goals and how each one affects the performing group. If the teacher didn't accomplish short-term goals 1 and 2, then the students would not be ready for contest or contest would be less than productive. The students also would be aware of the specific dates for completion and they would be responsible for helping meet short-term goal 3 and long-term goal.

This Goal Sheet illustrated to students that the teacher had to organize each day and week into student-focused rehearsals. Moreover, the teacher had to communicate to students their responsibility in achieving these goals by being focused, attentive, and cooperative in order for the group to reach the day's goals. As you recall previously, the instructor decided not to grade non-achievement activities such as attitude or attendance. But, if students did not work to make each rehearsal productive, they may not learn all the music for which they were responsible. The message here: teachers cannot do their jobs, if the students didn't do theirs; likewise, they wouldn't be able to learn what they were supposed to learn if the teacher didn't structure each rehearsal for success and follow through.

Director long-term goal #1 involves an assessment of the students by having them play for the teacher individually, beginning April 13. Students should know, from the beginning, that they would be responsible for an individual performance. Additionally, by having them set personal goals for musical skills (Student goals 2 and 3), the teacher is developing a sense of self-ownership in the process of growing musically.

It is important that you give students a Performance Rubric at the beginning of the year and refer to it daily in rehearsal in order to establish what the performance levels 1 – 5 represent. Reenforcing the daily rubric helps students understand how they will be evaluated or graded when they perform their music for the teacher on an established date. Additionally, students would know which exact sections they would perform for the assessment and how many points each one was weighted.

Director long-term goals 2 and 3 are based upon the data from the student juries the previous year. It is necessary students see that the teacher selected two areas of improvement to address with the entire band. These two goals also demonstrate that using data to improves the teacher's instruction and to targets the two areas that were the group's area of weakness. Lastly, Director long-term goal 3 communicated to each student that the teacher would take time individually to provide feedback on their musical skills and help them self-assess their progress in developing their musical skills.

WRITING STUDENT-ORIENTED GOALS

Now let's look at the Student Goals shown in Illustration 6. Do you notice there are four types: General, Music Skill, Theory and Listening?

ILLUSTRATION 6
STUDENT GOALS

Student Goals: Now it is your turn. What are several short- or long-term goals you would like to work on this quarter based upon the data from your performances and first semester listening and written theory final? Be as specific as you can and be sure to follow through.

1. General- Turn in all paper work on time and work on writing a better weekly planning sheet and reflect every other day on weekly progress.
2. Music skill- Learn the chromatic scale from low G below the staff to high G above the staff, using all alternate fingering and maintaining same tone quality throughout the scale.
3. Music skill- Practice sight-reading out of the sight-reading study book three times a week, performing two six-bar phrases focusing on key, time, how loud, and how fast
4. Theory Goal- Learn to recognize intervals on paper from a minor 2nd to major 7th, writing two quizzes a week on the computer at ninety percent accuracy.
5. Listening Goal- Learn to identify all major and perfect intervals on listening quizzes on the computer once a week with at ninety-five percent accuracy..

It was discovered that having students select the specific skills they needed to work on individually encouraged them to take responsibility for learning the goal and move toward mastery. Students would have been taught how to use the data from previous playing and written activities to set their goals. See chapter 9 for more information about teaching students to use data.

Students also needed to realize how to prioritize goals. People cannot work on everything at once (including the teacher), so it is necessary to select the goals that are most important for success. The sample Student Goals shows an example of specific and attainable student goals. These goals are not graded; however, by having students select their areas of weakness, they will understand that they will be accountable for their learning by semester's end.

Earlier in chapter 2, it was mentioned that the music department decided to develop clear learning targets in two areas:

1. **Student Musical Understanding** (SMU), which consists of listening (aural) music theory, music terms/ vocabulary, and genres.
2. **Student Performance Skills** (SPS), which consist of skills demonstrated through playing or singing.

We were able to incorporate clear learning targets into our grading practice only after we were able to articulate what skills we valued in our department. We didn't think we could develop complete musicians if we developed performance skills only; we thought it was necessary to develop both performance and musical understanding skills. Since we valued both these skill areas, we wanted to measure student growth in listening and written theory, in addition to performance, and provide a grade for each. The underlying assumption: students need to understand their strengths and weaknesses in order to select goals to work on.

To this end, our music department had to determine what skills the students should learn, how we would assess those skills, and how we would communicate to the students what level of skill (1-5) they were on. We determined what year we would assess each skill, when it would be taught, and what type of assessment would be used to measure the skill. The students would use the fall and first semester data about their performance and musical understanding skills to select the areas they needed to work on. More important, both the student and the teacher had established a clear skill level (1-5) for each area as a starting point. By establishing the starting point, we could measure their growth toward mastery and establish a numerical measurement of their growth. You don't know where you are or how much farther you have to go unless you know where you started.

SELECTING STUDENT MUSICAL UNDERSTANDING (SMU) SKILLS AND KNOWLEDGE

Look closely at how we selected the **Student Musical Understanding** (SMU) skills that consist of listening (aural), music theory, music terms/vocabulary, and genres. First, we had each member of the department bring music scores from the past two years of performances. We then wrote down all the terms, intervals, genres, vocabulary, keys, written theory and listening skills students needed to be able to play these songs.

You are probably wondering why two years of scores? The reason: we thought two years represented our unintended curriculum. We wanted to see if both years were similar in the level and skills needed to perform the music. Two years of information also would provide us with an idea of which skills were foundational and repeated from year-to year. We also didn't want to guess—rather, we wanted to base our skills on data from the past.

We discovered the necessary skills were similar from year-to-year, and we had *not clearly stated* to the students what skills we believed were important to be able to perform the music. It helped our department realize which skills should be our priority and which ones would be less of a focus. Once the skills were identified, we decided when and how we would assess them. Look at the example (see Illustration 7), and you will see columns for each of the musical skills we discovered from the two years of music and additional skills not in the music that we believed were needed for students to become Independent Musicians Creating Quality Performances (IMCQP). A blank Skills/Knowledge Template is shown here, but more detailed information can be found in *Scale Your Way to Music Assessment*.

The template in Illustration 7 has been organized into five columns. Since the focus of this book is on grading, the focus will be only on the columns that apply to grading or evaluation. Each area will be discussed in detail in each chapter in which you will be asked to complete that portion of the template.

1. Musical skills/vocabulary
2. Volume/reference
3. Year taught
4. Year tested
5. Objective
6. Assessment type—Written (W), listening (L), Individual Performance (IP), Summative (Sum) Assessments performed to determine the overall effectiveness of an educational program. Formative (F) Ongoing assessments within an educational program whose purpose is to improve the program as it progresses, Department Final (DF).

ILLUSTRATION 7

SKILL/KNOWLEDGE TEMPLATE

Skill/Knowledge	Volume #	YR Taught	YR Tested	Objective #						
					W	L	IP	S	F	DF
					W	L	IP	S	F	DF
					W	L	IP	S	F	DF
					W	L	IP	S	F	DF
					W	L	IP	S	F	DF
					W	L	IP	S	F	DF
					W	L	IP	S	F	DF
					W	L	IP	S	F	DF
					W	L	IP	S	F	DF
					W	L	IP	S	F	DF
					W	L	IP	S	F	DF
					W	L	IP	S	F	DF
					W	L	IP	S	F	DF
					W	L	IP	S	F	DF

Let's look at each column and how it keeps the students and the teacher focused on clear learning targets. In the first column, Skill/Knowledge, we would have listed listening (aural), music theory, music terms/vocabulary, and genres that had appeared in our music or we thought were vital to creating Independent Musicians Creating Quality Performances. Although we would write down everything from the music, it did not necessarily mean that we were going to assess the skill or knowledge formally. Remember the phrase from the assessment book:

ASSESS WHAT YOU VALUE AND VALUE WHAT YOU ASSESS

This phrase allowed us to understand that we should focus our assessments on the skills we valued.

Now look at column 2 Volume #. We realized when we wrote all the terms and theory from our music, there was absolutely no way we could teach all of what was needed without using a theory workbook and software program. We believed that music vocabulary and theory should be taught in context from the podium, but students also needed a way to practice the skills on their own. This addition of a theory workbook for each student that would complement what we were doing in rehearsal allowed us to ensure that each student received the necessary independent practice. We also purchased a software program to accompany the workbook from which students could practice skills without being graded. They could also take practice listening and written theory tests on their own, with the motivation that they were responsible for learning the skills taught in class. Since students love video games, the software made learning music skills fun. At the end of the module, students would get a score that we would not see. If they didn't get 100 percent, they would go back and try the test again until they earned a perfect score indicating mastery.

In addition to the software program and workbook, we developed short quizzes and practice worksheets that were posted on our department Web page. Students could access the page and practice skills without having to use the school's software. Again, this practice was not graded and we would not see the results. If a student did not think they understood the theory, we made ourselves available to help them one-on-one. You would be surprised how many students came in for a brief, individual tutoring session. Students who were strong musicians who could perform complex music would say, "I never knew what was behind the music I played. This makes the music so much more interesting."

You are probably asking yourself, "But, how did the teachers measure student growth and how did the students understand where they were in their skill development?" If you look at the example below, you will see what we evaluated at the end of both semesters. Yes, we did evaluate the students' progress in order to provide feedback, but the quizzes and other assessments had a very small weight.

We wanted the grade at the end of the semester to be weighted more than at the beginning of the semester to encourage practice with no fear of failure or a failing grade.

After receiving the results of their performances and semester listening and written theory final, the students would select their weakest areas on which to concentrate. The grade they received was based upon how much growth they made from the pre-test to the first semester. On the second semester test, we would grade based upon the growth from semester one to semester two. This model allowed us to have a differentiated grading system based upon individual growth in performance and theory skills.

Below are sample Year 1 Written and the Listening Skills that were based upon the two years of past music performed and the additional skills needed to be Independent Musicians Creating Quality Performances

YEAR 1 WRITTEN TEST

Volume 1, Unit 1*   Staff, Notes, and Pitches

Volume 1, Unit 2   Note Values, Time Signatures, and Rests

Volume 1, Unit 3   Time Signatures, Ties and Slurs

Volume 1, Unit 4   Repeats, Eighth Notes, and Dotted-Quarter Notes

Volume 1, Unit 5   Dynamics, Tempo Marks, Articulation, D.C. and D.S.

Volume 1, Unit 6   Flats, Sharps, Naturals, Whole/Half Steps, and Enharmonics

Volume 2, Unit 7   Tetrachords, Scales, and Key Signatures

Volume 2, Unit 8   Key Signatures, Chromatics, and Intervals

Volume 2, Unit 9   Intervals and *Solfége*

*Volumes and Units refer to the theory workbook.

YEAR 1 LISTENING TEST

Interval Recognition-Visual (ascending only)

Correct Notation-Listening

Rhythm and Notes

Rhythm-Visual

Scale Recognition-Visual/Listening

Intervals-Not Visual

Triads-Not Visual

Intervals-Visual

SELECTING STUDENT PERFORMANCE SKILLS (SPS) AND KNOWLEDGE

Look more closely at how we selected the **Student Performance Skills** (SPS) that consist of skills demonstrated through playing or singing and are divided into eight categories:

Tone Quality— Resonance, Control, Clarity, Focus, Consistency, and Warmth

Intonation— Accuracy of Printed Pitches

Rhythm— Accuracy of Notes and Rest Values, Duration, Pulse, Steadiness, and Correctness of Meters

Technique (Facility/Accuracy) — Artistry, Attacks, Releases, Control of Ranges, Musical and/or Mechanical Skills

Interpretation, Musicianship— Style, Phrasing, Tempo, Dynamics, and Emotional Involvement

Diction— Vocal

Bowing— Strings

Articulation— Winds

Other Performance Factors— Choice of Literature, Appropriate Appearance, Poise, Posture, General Conduct, Mannerisms, and Facial Expression (Vocal), Memory Scales, Intervals, Triads

The rubric in Illustration 8 is from the National Federation of High Schools for rating musical performance skills. This rubric is the same one that the State of Illinois uses for its state contest. Using a consistent rubric is important so that students understand the expectations at the school, state and/or national level.

ILLUSTRATION 8

PERFORMANCE RUBRIC

NFHS Music SOLO Adjudication Form

Program/Event # _____ Room_____   Order of Appearance _____ Time_____

Event _____ Student Name _____

School Name _____ Class_____ School Code _____

SCORE   AREA OF CONCERN AND COMMENTS

SCORE	AREA OF CONCERN AND COMMENTS
____.____	**Tone Quality** resonance, control, clarity, focus, consistency, and warmth
____.____	**Intonation** accuracy to printed pitches
____.____	**Rhythm** accuracy of note and rest values, duration, pulse, steadiness, and correctness of meters (Indent)
____.____	**Technique (facility/accuracy)** artistry, attacks, releases, control of ranges, and musical/ mechanical skill
____.____	**Interpretation, Musicianship** style, phrasing, tempo, dynamics, and emotional involvement
____.____	**Diction - Vocal** **Bowing – Strings** **Articulation – Winds**
____.____	**Performance Factors** Choice of literature, appropriate appearance, poise, posture, general conduct, mannerisms, facial expression, and vocal memory
____.____	**Scales** fingerings, key, tone, intonation, rhythm, tempo, and (memory-EVERYONE) **Instrumental and Strings** two scales one chromatic **Vocal** One major scale - One form of natural/harmonic/melodic minor One major triad - ne form of minor/diminished/augmented

___.____ **Total** Circle Rating Do Not Round Up	Division I (Superior) = 40 to 36.0 = 5 - A superior performance - outstanding in nearly every detail Division II (Excellent) = 35.9 to 28.0 = 4 - An excellent performance — minor defects Division III (Good) = 27.9 to 20.0 = 3 - A good performance -lacking finesse and/or interpretation Division IV (Fair) = 19.9 to 12 = 2 - A fair performance — basic weaknesses Division V (Poor) = 11.9 to 8.00 = 1 - A poor performance — unsatisfactory

To select the Student Performance Skills (SPS) and knowledge that we valued, the music department followed the same process that we used to identify the skills and knowledge of Student Musical Understanding (SMS). Using music scores from the past two years, we wrote down every rhythm, scale, interval, note range in each piece, tempo markings, accent—in other words, any skill or knowledge that a musician would need in order to perform the pieces we had played or sung. We listed what we wanted students to be able to do and know in the Skills and Knowledge template Illustration 7 and then the music department decided when these skills or knowledge would be taught and how they would be assessed. Below are samples Year 1 Band and Choir Performance Expectations.

YEAR 1 BAND

- Perform individual solo at contest or in front of the band for rating or grade. (Required).
- Perform in a small group (ensemble) at contest for rating. (Required).
- Perform individual solo (see list), sight-read and (play/sing) scales and triads (in May (Jury).
- Perform scales (Concert Pitch) C, F, Bb, Eb, Ab, Db, Gb, G, D—Sing C, F, G.
- Perform all three forms of minor scales, natural, harmonic, and melodic on keys above.
- Perform playing and singing major, minor, and diminished triads on the keys above.
- Perform the rhythms and rests (see list) by sight-singing and playing.
- Perform 4/4 –3/4- 2/4 - meters in sight-singing and playing.

YEAR 1 CHOIR

- Perform individual solo at contest for rating or comment. (Optional)
- Perform in a small group (ensemble) at contest for rating or comment. (Required)
- Perform on piano and sing these scales: C, F, G.
- Perform in the Large Group IHSA Contest every other year.
- Perform three choir concerts.
- Perform playing and singing major, minor, and diminished triads in the keys above.

DETERMINING A GRADE

Let's return to the question in chapter 3, Assessing Your Current Grading System:
Are your grades a mathematical average of all your assignments?

This question is posed because averaging grades during a quarter or semester goes against the ultimate purpose of grading, which is to communicate individual student performance or theory growth or achievement. Grades, especially in music, should not be averaged. In the early stages of learning musical skills, students will fail often, since musical skills develop over time. If you weight all assignments and performances the same, the grade at the end of the term does not accurately communicate the student level of achievement or musical growth. Averaging is also very non motivating to students who may give up or become frustrated during the semester when they realize it is not possible to improve their grades after a rough start at the beginning of the school year. Most online-grading programs allow teachers to post assignments that do not count toward the final grade. Students still can see their level of achievement without having it affect the end-of-term grade. If you believe you must average grades, the grades earned at the beginning of the semester should have very little weight. The level of student skill, knowledge, and individual musical growth at the end of the semester are the most important consideration when assigning a grade.

ASSESSING STUDENT GROWTH AND PROVIDING FEEDBACK

To provide a baseline for students' skills growth, students initially took a pre-test to measure their performance skills. This test allowed the teacher to know the performance level of each student at the beginning of the semester. You will also notice on the rubric (See Illustration 8) that numbers and not grades are used to show where the student is in his skill development. We spent a large amount of time describing each of the eight categories and creating examples of the levels of expectation so that students had an in-depth understanding of what the numbers represented. Eventually, the numbers would be converted into a grade, but only at the end of the term, which would allow time for students to advance in their musical skills.

At the end of each semester, both student and teacher would evaluate the progress based upon the data from individual performances. Then, the student would set new goals for the next term. During the semester, teachers made sure they heard students perform individually both in class as well as outside of class so we could monitor their progress and provide guided feedback on their development of the selected skills. Although hearing students individually outside of class takes time, it is a necessary part of being a music teacher and the only way to provide one-on-one feedback on a variety of musical skills. Teachers cannot assess students solely from the podium, nor can they depend on software packages to be the only methods of assessing student skills and providing feedback. Students need to have the personalized instruction and assessment that can only come from a music teacher in a face-to-face session.

Our music department made a commitment to hear students individually several times a semester. For example, students would perform music individually before each concert. We also would have them come in for short performances of the skills they had selected as goals. During those meetings, we would help them understand where they were in the development of their musical skills. Additionally, we would suggest further ways to continue to improve those skills.

Furthermore, the department had an extensive peer-assessment program in which students would play or sing for one another, focusing on the skill they had selected. Their peers would provide comments and suggestions for improvement. The peer-assessment program required a period of time to develop because we wanted our students to understand how to use musical terms in their comments and suggestions. In other words, you must train students how to be good assessors and feedback providers.

Let's sum up how we combined grading and assessment. We selected specific skills that the department valued. Students then took a pre-test in performance skills, listening, and written theory to provide a baseline so we could measure the amount of skill growth each student made. Based upon this information, teachers and students analyzed student strengths and weaknesses and set goals. Numerous opportunities for practice and feedback from directors, peers, and outside evaluators were offered. At the end of the semester, a culminating assessment allowed students to demonstrate the skills learned over the course of the term.

Ultimately, what students can do with their musical skills and knowledge is what really matters if educators hope to create future independent musicians. The ability to perform music with understanding and emotional feeling at a high level of mastery are what we want students to know and be able to do. Before moving on, let's reflect on what you have discovered as a result of reading this chapter.

Consider the following question: What changes would you make to your current grading practices?

_____

_____

_____

_____

_____

_____

_____

ADMINISTRATIVE PERSPECTIVE

The State of Illinois has adopted a model of teacher performance evaluation that is based upon a The Framework for Teaching by Charlotte Danielson. The framework describes four levels of teaching proficiency with Level 4 being the highest. If one looks at what distinguishes the characteristics of a high-performing teacher, one will see that student involvement, independence, and ownership of the learning process are the key. To move to the highest level of expertise in teaching, students need to be in the "driver's seat" and thus in control of their own learning.

Teaching students how to set learning goals and to work toward mastery is a key factor in creating student ownership of their learning in the classroom. It is reasonable to point out when administrators visit a classroom, they want to see students who know what they need to know and understand the process of how they are going to get there.

CHAPTER 6
ATTRIBUTION THEORY: MASTERY VERSUS PERFORMANCE

As the music faculty reviewed research about grading and student achievement, they discovered Bernard Weiner's Attribution Theory (1974, 1986). The basic premise of the theory is that people attribute success or failure to many factors that include the perception of ability, effort, task difficulty, and luck. Weiner categorized people into two groups: those who were either mastery-oriented or performance-oriented.

If we view students in our music classes as fitting into one of the Attribution Theory's two groups, mastery-oriented students would seek to *improve* their competence while performance-oriented students would seek to *prove* their competence. Students who are mastery-orientated would tend to see the value of practice and effort in learning a musical skill, whereas, students who are performance-oriented would tend to see ability as finite—a person is either musically talented or not—and would not see the correlation of practice and effort with musical success.

The following chart displayed in Illustration 9 by Marilla D. Svinicki delineates the characteristics of mastery-oriented students and performance-oriented students. *Student Goal Orientation, Motivation, and Learning* (Marilla D. Svinicki, 2005).

ILLUSTRATION 9
MASTERY VERSUS PERFORMANCE

Mastery Oriented Students	Performance Oriented Students
Main interest is in learning the skill/content.	Main interest is in appearing competent or better than others regardless of level achieved.
Willing to take on difficult tasks beyond present capability.	Sticks to tasks that are familiar, known quantities.
Views mistakes as learning opportunities.	Views mistakes as evidence of lack of competence and therefore to be avoided.

Music teachers strive daily to help students achieve high-level musical skills. To that end, understanding the difference in student orientation may prompt teachers to examine the types of tasks we ask of students and the type of learning environment we create in the classroom. Let's look at mastery first.

MASTERY-ORIENTED STUDENTS

When we began to see the two types of learners, it became evident that we needed to look at both our achievement tasks and what types of students we had in our department. What could we do to set the stage for success for the mastery-oriented student?

Mastery-oriented students believe that they have some control over factors related to learning. They believe they can learn, that hard work and effort pays off, and they have or can acquire strategies that will help them learn. They don't give up easily when a learning task challenges them. Department members discussed these traits at great length, and we agreed that these were the qualities in our students that we wanted our learning environment and new grading system to foster.

PERFORMANCE-ORIENTED STUDENTS

When we realized that our lower-skilled students were the same ones who might drop out, it helped us to understand that they were often performance-oriented. Students with this orientation saw learning as something beyond their control. They tended to equate learning with ability, and after several failed attempts to learn something, they decided they couldn't do it and quit. They were reluctant to expend effort because they believed they wouldn't be able to learn the musical skills we were asking. They thought they just didn't have what it takes. As our music department discussion continued, we made similar comments about how often we heard our students blaming outside influences and not taking personal responsibility for their actions. We also found that these students were more likely to complain about the grade they received than the mastery-oriented students. One reason for the complaining, we realized, was the lack of clear learning targets that the student could aim for. This lack of clarity created frustration and led to students dropping the class, becoming complacent, or undermining the efforts of other students. What we needed was to create a system in which we clearly articulated the level we desired for students and then give clear and timely feedback about where they were in the task. We also wanted to give the feedback in a non evaluative and a positive manner. This change was a major step for the department in developing an environment in which a high level of achievement is expected and effort and persistence are rewarded.

We had to think about how well we could balance mastery and performance goals. Students must perform in our classes, but we could emphasize how the activities and assignments we evaluated offered an opportunity to feel a sense of accomplishment. Equally important is how we would demonstrate that effort does make a difference. We could lecture the students about the value of hard work, but would they really listen? Wouldn't it be more effective to design activities in which the students could discover what they could do once they "put their minds to it"?

COLLABORATION VERSUS COMPETITION

The research about collaborative and competitive reward structures seems to indicate that minimizing competition and rewarding collaboration results in better learning. (Johnson, D. & Johnson, R, 1985). Education's movement of grading from norm-referenced and comparative to criterion-referenced and individual achievement-based will also help move the students' focus away from how they compare to others to how much progress they have made and how much further they need to go. Even the shift to portfolio grading as opposed to summative tests as the basis for grades plays a role in shifting student attention toward higher levels of achievement.

One can understand we tend to compare our grades to others' grades, or we want to see how many other A's or B's were dispensed, but is that what we value in music? Music involves a collaboration of students of different talents and skill levels working for a common goal. It becomes vital in a group activity to consider two types of comparisons: student to self and student to group. The first type, student to self, is based upon demonstrating to students the amount of growth they have made over time. Student self-reflection was an important part of that process.

Knowledge of an individual's skills growth, however, must be balanced with the fact that, in a group activity, students need to achieve a certain skill level so they can contribute positively to the group. We tried to address this issue by having students do peer assessments, so students could understand how they performed in relation to their peers. Teacher assessments also provided information to students about where they stood in relation to the group. In chapter 9, there is a discussion about how to use data to show students where they are, in relation to the overall departmental student data.

Providing students with information about how individual achievement relates to the group is crucial to developing a collaborative learning environment. When teachers shared information about the achievement growth a student had made individually and the progress the group had made during the semester, the students were very motivated. They were able to celebrate not only their individual success, but also the group success as well.

More important, students could better understand where to focus individual and group efforts. Having this understanding alleviated some of the competitiveness that occurs among student musicians. Instead, the focus was now on what everyone needed to do individually for the group to improve. In other words, the group was only as strong as the weakest individual's skills and ability. If a student wanted the group to move forward, then that student now knew exactly what needed to be accomplished both individually and as a group in order to improve.

Although it seems simple, what made this approach so powerful was that we focused on numbers (Levels 1-5 on the rubric) and not grades. Centering on the level of expected achievement helped students see their accomplishments as a positive part of the bigger picture.

At times, selecting and ranking musicians is necessary. This sorting may occur when selecting higher-skilled groups or during state or national competitions. Ranking is not inherently bad, if it is used for the right purpose; it also can be very motivating, especially to the performance-oriented student. However, ranking students should never be linked to grades in the music classroom. Competition should not be encouraged, especially when students are learning new skills. This process brings out the worst in not only the individual, but also it undermines any sense of camaraderie or cohesion in a group.

ADMINISTRATIVE PERSPECTIVE

Administrators would love to foster a mastery-oriented learning environment throughout the school. Think of the possibilities if students could see the results of their efforts in learning!

Before we can expect students to adopt this philosophy, however, we as educators should examine our own views about learning. Faculty members are, in general, more interested in appearing competent or better than others? Should they only stick to what they know or have done in the past? Do they view mistakes as evidence of incompetence and something that they want to avoid at all costs? If teachers don't model the behaviors of mastery-orientation such as viewing mistakes as opportunities for learning, demonstrating a willingness to take on difficult tasks, and admitting that they are not the source of all knowledge in their subjects, how will they be able to affect the perception of learning for their students? Having honest conversations about these questions are necessary if we hope to develop the type of atmosphere where learning can truly happen.

CHAPTER 7
TAKING OWNERSHIP FOR SUCCESS

I still remember my first practice sheet in grade school. It looked something similar to the one below:

Name_____ School_____

Day and Date	Time Practiced	Parent Signature
Monday		
Tuesday		
Wednesday		
Thursday		
Friday		
Saturday		
Saturday		
Sunday		

Remembering still the finagling my parents into signing that I had practiced, even if I had not. Probably I forged a few signatures. Motivated mainly out of fear that my grade would be adversely affected if the practice sheet did not indicate that I had practiced thirty minutes a day. And if I didn't secure a parental signature. My youthful perception may be that the teacher didn't care about how their students practiced, how many glasses of water they retrieved during the practice session, or if they chose to play only the music they liked and not the pieces that were challenging. The following is an anecdotal account of the author's regarding practice, procrastination, and a parent's signature:

> I did know, however, that a value was placed on the number of minutes and a parent signature, and I was determined to make sure I complied. I was also a procrastinator. I waited until the last minute to prepare music for concerts, contest, auditions, or tryouts—you name it, I waited until the last minute. Even as adults, we know people who have developed the undesirable habit of procrastination. Fortunately, I was able to overcome my earlier tendency, and thus, I wanted to create a way for my students to learn to work consistently on time management, an essential skill necessary for the long-term effort needed to develop musical skills.

As discussed in chapter 6, learners can be thought of as being in one of two camps, mastery-oriented or performance-oriented. Performance-oriented students tend to be your procrastinators. They will blame and try to justify why they didn't learn what they should have because they waited or procrastinated. To help these students change this way of behaving, we developed a weekly planning sheet that is not graded for content and does not require a parent's signature. The planning sheet in Illustration 10 below is designed so students can write when they would practice on and in what specific areas they would work. Have the student include a start and end time. They can become good only so fast.

ILLUSTRATION 10

PLANNING SHEET

SAMPLE PLANNING SHEET

This plan sheet should focus on the two major performances for Quarter 3. Times and dates should be accurate. <u>Please use specific language to indicate the focus of your practice.</u>

Name_____Due Date_____ Student ID_____

LUCK – There is no such thing as luck; only the ability to
<u>L</u>ABOR – <u>U</u>NDER – <u>C</u>ORRECT – <u>K</u>NOWLEDGE

Friday – Date____Start Time_____End Time_____

Band/Perc./Ensemble/Solo/Lesson/Scale   Section/Measures What is the focus?

Saturday - Date_____ Start Time_____End Time_____

Band/Perc./Ensemble/Solo/Lesson/Scale   Section/Measures What is the focus?

Sunday - Date_____ Start Time_____End Time_____

Band/Perc./Ensemble/Solo/Lesson/Scale   Section/Measures What is the focus?

Monday - Date_____ Start Time_____End Time_____

Band/Perc./Ensemble/Solo/Lesson/Scale   Section/Measures What is the focus?

Tuesday - Date_____ Start Time_____End Time_____

Band/Perc./Ensemble/Solo/Lesson/Scale   Section/Measures What is the focus?

Wednesday - Date_____ Start Time_____End Time_____

Band/Perc./Ensemble/Solo/Lesson/Scale   Section/Measures What is the focus?

Thursday – Date_____ Start Time_____End Time_____

Band/Percussion./Ensemble/Solo/Lesson/Scale Section/Measures What is the focus?

The point is to have students who have no intention of practicing on a certain day to write *no practice* without a grade consequence. If they wanted to write for seven days "no practice" and provide a reason, that, too, is okay, but then refer back to their original goal sheet. If they had performance and musical skill goals, in addition to the music that would be performed for the teacher by a given date, then one could easily reply on their planning sheet:

> I noticed that you are not practicing, so how will you reach the individual and group goals you committed to for Quarter 3?

The obvious intent here is for the student to be aware of taking responsibility for their own musical progress.

ENCOURAGING A REFLECTIVE LOOP

When earning a counseling degree, I learned a technique called the reflective loop. The process of reflection can best be illustrated by a graphic of a straight line followed by a loop that circles around and then rejoins the straight line (See Illustration 11). Think of the line as *time* and the loop as an *event* such as a performance, practice, rehearsal, or assessment. You will notice that the cycle repeats several times over the length of the time line as the students reflect back on their progress over time. Most of the events in the students' reflective loops were ungraded opportunities for feedback regarding skills.

> *Without reflection, we go blindly on our way, creating more unintended consequences, and failing to achieve anything useful.*
>
> —Margret J. Wheatley

ILLUSTRATION 11

REFLECTIVE LOOP

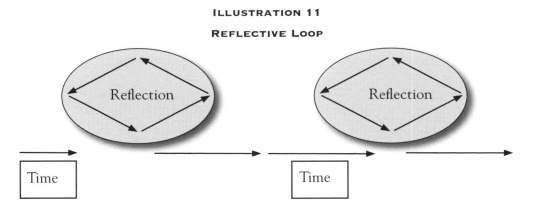

The loop represents how students should reflect on what has happened and then how they can adjust their plans based upon those reflections until the event occurs again. A Weekly Reflection sheet (see Illustration 12) encourages a reflective loop by having students compare what they planned to do in the Planning Sheet (see Illustration 10) against what they actually did. This process of reflection allows students to take responsibility for improving their skills weekly. Consider using the following phrase to encourage students to reflect honestly:

"The worst lie you can tell is to yourself."

ILLUSTRATION 12

WEEKLY REFLECTION

SAMPLE WEEKLY REFLECTION

Name_____ Student #_____Week Beginning _____

Two Days until you play your solo with piano!
Zero Days until your ensemble starts playing for the band
Nine Days until Contest.

How many times did you practice your solo?

How many times outside of band did your ensemble practice?
Remember you are to meet once a week.

You were asked to be able to count your solo aloud in tempo. Can you do it? Yes or No
If you marked *Yes* and cannot do it in band or for me, then you will have to come back and try again.

Can you play your chromatic or rudiments without mistakes up and down. Yes or No
If you say *Yes* and cannot do it in band or for me, then you will have to come back and try again.

Can you play your scales or rudiments up and down without mistakes? Yes or No
If you say *Yes* and cannot do it in band or for me, then you will have to come back and try again.

You will play with your piano player next week. Can you play straight through your solo after having it for the past eight weeks? Yes or No

If you say *Yes* and cannot do it in band or for me, then you will have to come back and try again.

What three tuning notes will you use? 1.____2.____3._____ Remember to use notes from your solo that you hold out or play numerous times. One note should always be concert Bb.

What did you not get done that you planned to complete this week?

What did you accomplish this week?

What will you do differently next week?

Some of you are probably asking yourself " What did you grade the student on?"?

We did give students a small number of points for completing the Planning Sheet with specific information and points for the Reflection Sheet for honest reflections. Since the faculty valued the skills of time management and reflection as essential to student musical growth, we did have a small portion of the grade dedicated to these musical behaviors. Students always had the opportunity to rewrite sheets, and thus, no student received a zero for the assignment.

That brings us to the "no zero policy." We did not give zeros; instead, we would allow multiple chances to complete an assignment. Why? The main idea of developing a skill is to encourage students to practice with the goal of moving toward mastery. Planning and reflection allows that practice to be purposeful and efficiently move students forward toward attaining their goals. What would a teacher be reinforcing or teaching students with a low grade or zero? Teachers should want students to succeed and do everything to support their efforts. But, teachers should not support avoidance of responsibility. Students do not intuitively understand their role in the process, and as educators, we have to show them how to succeed so that success becomes a habit. Answer the following questions to get the discussion started about how to create a climate of student ownership in your department.

What is more important, giving a grade or allowing students multiple opportunities for feedback? Why?

_____

_____

What are the plusses and minuses of creating a system in the music classroom for developing time management skills or helping students connect the results of their effort and their long-term goals? If you do not have such as system, explain how you plan to help your students develop into independent musicians?

_____

_____

How do you currently motivate students to be self-directed learners? Is your system effective?

_____

_____

Do your students wait until the last minute to develop skills? If so, is that something you want to change?

_____

_____

ADMINISTRATIVE PERSPECTIVE

By encouraging students to be responsible in engaging the learning process through a reflective loop, teachers are handing their students the keys to success. But, student responsibility doesn't mean we "dig a hole" for students that is so deep they cannot get out. This author has heard many teachers resist the concept of not giving zeroes because they think students need to learn a lesson. Unfortunately, the lesson they learn is to give up when confronted with an insurmountable task.

Motivational research supports the notion that students are driven by what are called the three C's: a feeling of Competence; an opportunity for Choice in their learning; and a personal Connection, whether it be to the teacher or the task. By embedding goal setting into a course curriculum, you are developing that sense of competence as students start to see effort and persistence pay off. By individualizing the goals, you are reinforcing the view that they have a choice about which skills they will work on and multiple opportunities to demonstrate those skills. Finally, the relationship that you will build with your students as a teacher/coach who truly wants students to succeed will result in increased student motivation to work toward the goals of the course. Please consult the readings about motivating students in the work of Edward L. Deci and Carol Dweck.

CHAPTER 8
CHANGING THE CULTURE

If you want to change the culture, you will have to start by changing the organization.

—Mary Douglas

After reading Bernard Weiner's Attribution Theory (1974, 1986) and the research on mastery-oriented students, we knew we had to change our music department's learning environment. But, what would this environment look like that would develop the characteristics of mastery-oriented students? We settled on two ideas taken from the literature. We wanted to create a learning environment in which students are motivated to engage in behaviors that:

1. value to them; and
2. provide them with a reasonable expectation to succeed.

In this new learning environment, we would choose tasks that our students valued, and we structure the learning so their probability of success was reasonable. In addition, we would support student efforts while they worked on tasks or skills so that they were encouraged by their progress.

One way to confirm what we thought was to ask the students what they wanted from our performing groups and what motivated them to want to learn music and take our classes. We created a student survey and had them anonymously answer the questions. We wanted honest answers and didn't want students to fear negative consequences if they were candid about our grading or music classes. The teachers in the department gave the survey on the same day and explained that we were seriously considering changing the department grading policies. After the explanation, we put a box in the front of the room for them to drop their surveys and then left the room, leaving our department secretary to monitor the room until the class bell rang. Feel free to duplicate the Student Grading Survey below and allow your students to give you feedback.

Student Grading Survey

Why did you originally want to play an instrument or sing?

_____

_____

What motivates you to work on developing musical skills?

_____

_____

What motivates you to try new tasks?

_____

_____

What does NOT motivate you?

_____

_____

Do you believe the current grading system motivates you to work on developing musical skills? Yes or No. Explain.

_____

_____

Do you believe the current system is fair to all students?

_____

_____

What is more important to you,

the grade you get

Or

the experience of making music in a group? Explain your answer.

_____

_____

Can you imagine what we thought when we left the room and waited for their answers. The faculty was full of apprehension, but also excited to read the answers and get direct insight into how and what the students thought about our grading and what motivated them.

Answer these two questions below as a department.

1. If we surveyed our students about our grading policies, what would their answers be?
2. If the answers pointed out major flaws in our current system, would we change them?

The answers we got back from the students were incredibly honest and seemed to be written with a great deal of thought. The students commented repeatedly that grades were important and gave reasons such as GPA, class rank, or transcripts that would be sent to colleges; what was more enlightening, however, was that they didn't mind getting a low grade if they could see it coming and if they understood clearly what they had been graded on. Eighty percent of the students wanted to be graded on their individual musical growth and not the musical growth of the group. In addition, they wanted to be able to work on skills on which they were weak and not generic large-group skill development exercises they had already mastered. Seventy-five percent wanted a specific list of skills to work on that was tailored to them. They stated repeatedly that they wanted to improve their weak skill areas and needed teacher guidance in understanding what exercises, books, solos, or etudes they needed to work on to improve targeted weak areas. After reading the comments and discussing them, it was very clear to us that we would have to change the learning environment and that we had the students' blessing and encouragement.

But, we must communicate with the parents and the administration as well? Do you remember in the introduction when our principal agreed to work with us on changing the grading policies of the department? The results of the student survey were explained to Dr. Joe and we shared the ideas we had with him. It was a great discussion that ended with us devising a plan to involve the parents and students equally. If the parents didn't "buy in," then they would not support their children or us in developing the program. Communicating why we were changing the grading system and how it would become more student-centered would help us gain the support from the stake holders that we needed.

CHANGING THE CULTURE OF THE REHEARSAL

We have already discussed the importance of prioritizing musical skills in chapter 3 of this book, but it is necessary to elaborate more about how creating a list of skills changed our learning environment. When we first began developing our list of skills with student encouragement, the task seemed overwhelming. Once we started, however, it was really quite easy. Do you remember how we used the past two years of scores to begin the list? When it came time to show the students the performance, listening, and written music theory skills, we had prioritized as learning targets; the students understood why we had selected those skills. Three-fourths of the students had played the music we selected. When we showed them why we had selected these skills that were related to the music they had performed, they understood the rationale. This understanding created student support and desire to learn the skills t we would teach and test.

So, how did we change the classroom culture? Simple, the department moved from a teacher-driven learning environment to one that was driven by the students. We changed from teaching classes populated with students who had no understanding about the expectations or learning objectives to teaching classes in which the students not only understood, but also the learning targets for the group and the individual. They also knew where their skill level was in developing the skills needed to move the group forward. WOW! We were able to create an environment rooted in the philosophy of shared responsibility for moving the group and the individual ahead.

Creating this shared responsibility changed our teaching relationships with the students. It was no longer the band, choir, or orchestra directors pressuring students to improve; instead, the relationship was more collegial, or one in which teachers and students were working together for a common purpose. Can you imagine what our administration thought when they observed us teaching? In the pre-observation meeting, we would explain our goal for the day, how we were going to move students forward toward achieving that goal and how we would measure progress at the end of the rehearsal. We could also show the administrator where each student was in developing the skills needed to perform that day's music. In addition, they also could see that the students understood their role in making the class an educational experience. What was most impressive to the administrators was that we could use data from individual student performances and daily rehearsals to improve our teaching. What a fantastic learning environment for both teacher and student!

DEVELOPING A TEACHER LEARNING ENVIRONMENT

In many of the educational books we read, the focus was on classrooms as student-centered. The department realized, however, that we needed to create a teacher learning environment as well. What were the characteristics of a classroom in which the teacher was also the learner? Once we had the focus of the department on skills, goals, student expectations, data from individual performances, and had created a shared rehearsal responsibility, we believed that we had begun to learn more about teaching. Yes, we began to see that by having an environment in which each steak holder (student, teacher, administration, parents) understood what their role was in improving our performing groups the individual musicians, the faculty believed they were beginning to better understand what teaching was all about. You may well say, "but weren't you teaching before?" Probably, in a very loose sense of the word, but we were most concerned about fixing mistakes over and over again without being able to "get to the music." That one word, "music," was why our students and we as teachers became involved in the experience of making and playing music. We wanted to make music and experience the emotions, and the phrasing involved in creating a musical experience. In other words, we longed to encounter the deeper meaning inherent in the music we were playing.

Let's take time to reflect on why you love and teach music. Answer the question below.

Why do I love music and why do I want others to share that feeling?

_____

_____

CREATING THE OPPORTUNITY FOR AESTHETIC EXPERIENCES

This author had a music teacher tell him at a workshop that one shouldn't judge a subjective art because it would ruin the aesthetic experience. He obviously had some baggage and did not understand that students cannot have an aesthetic experience or much of one, if they did not have the skills to perform the music in a way that gave life to all of the nuances in the music. Of course one might have such a feeling in a beautiful performance hall while listening to a concert or while studying a painting, but one will not have the deep personal experience if one is not actively involved at a very high level. The research describes this experience as one of focused concentration on what one is doing at the present.

We have talked to athletes, students, musicians, speakers, and teachers about the aesthetic experience. In almost every discussion, the person would observe they were performing or concentrating at a high level of understanding and skill. In that moment, something just "clicked" that gave them that incredible feeling that they rarely experience. To attain that highpoint, each person had to develop a high-level of skill and ability that allowed the individual to concentrate on or be totally "present in the moment" rather than focusing upon performing skills in isolation.

Describe an aesthetic experience you have had and share it with your department.

_____

_____

Changing your classroom focus from grades to one of developing the skills valued by your music department, you are creating an opportunity for you and your students to have that wonderful encounter with the aesthetic experience. Eventually, you will take the numbers and turn them into grades, but those grades will now clearly communicate where students are in the process of mastering those skills. What a feeling you will have when you change your old grading practices and provide your students with valuable information so they can improve as musicians and you can improve as a teacher.

ADMINISTRATIVE PERSPECTIVE

An earlier discussion touched on developing a shared relationship with your administration, but let's look more closely at how the perception of the music department changed as a result of the department's new practices. Once their grading and assessment system focused upon individual student-skill development and the teachers used that information to improve teaching and learning, their interactions with the administration were transformed.

Now the music faculty could show the administration that music was as relevant to the school community as the core curriculum and could evaluate and communicate student progress more clearly than the other departments. The music department became the leaders of change, not the inhibitors of change. Department members could have discussions about how they were using data to improve teaching and use that data to improve student learning.

The music faculty also could use the grading data and other assessment results to justify their programs. Defending programs is a constant issue for the arts that will not go away, especially when school budgets are limited. We need to show the connection of the arts to the other disciplines. We need to have similar grading standards and illustrate how music is essential in building skills that are needed for the twenty-first century. As a result of their leading educational change in their school, the music faculty could ask for more money, equipment, and/or resources because they could demonstrate their value to the school community. Furthermore, the number of grade and parent complaints dropped drastically. If there was a criticism, teachers could discuss the issue with the administration and parents, knowing they understood every aspect of the grading system.

We leave you to answer one more question.

How would your relationship change with your administration and parents if you altered the way you assessed and graded?

_____

_____

_____

CHAPTER 9
USING DATA TO CREATE A DIFFERENTIATED GRADING SYSTEM

One probably has never taught a class in which all the students were at the same performance level or level of understanding. Yet, most of us grade everyone on the same achievement or non-achievement activities. If you remember in chapter 8 how we changed our learning environment and how we motivated students, then you will understand how we developed a system in which each student had a different expectation for musical growth in the three different areas we valued: performance, listening, and written theory skills. It is not possible to compare a student who can play fourth or fifth grade-level music with excellent tone to a student who is in the same group but has minimal technical and musical skills if you have a single set of expectations for both. Still, all students should be expected to improve their skills, but in different ways. The reader may well respond, "But, I do that already with my effort and participation grades."

PAUSE

How can you grade effort and participation? Are you really able to objectively measure how hard or efficiently all your students work if you are not at each of their practice sessions? In addition, a skill that might take one student twenty minutes three times a week to accomplish, might take another student an hour five times a week to accomplish. Answer the following questions.

Have you ever had to work harder than someone else to reach the same skill level?

_____

_____

Have you ever been graded on effort or participation and were unsure about the fairness of the grade?

_____

_____

Would you like to be graded or evaluated on effort? For example, a fellow teacher spends twelve to fourteen hours a day at school compared to you who is much more efficient and who only spends eight hours a day at school. Unlike the other teacher, you spend one to two hours each evening, unbeknown to your principal, involved in schoolwork. Would you be upset if your principal gave the teacher who got less done but spent more time visibly at school a better rating? What if your students showed more musical growth and a higher level of understanding than the teacher who spent more time? Would that be fair?

It seems reasonable to suggest one would want to be judged on how much musical growth their students demonstrates and not on how much time a teacher spent at work. Think about your students and if you are grading on effort. Have you established, in writing, what your grading guidelines are for effort and how you will grade each student's efforts objectively?

Our music faculty sat down with each student and discussed what areas both teacher and student believed were areas in need of improvement and the timeline required to make desired musical growth. We learned that stating to the student what minimum amount of growth we expected the student to make that the student would only work to that level. We found that by not stating a minimum the students tended to make larger gains in skill since they were working to develop the skills not the amount of growth.

In order to measure student growth, you must have a baseline set of scores. Each student must have a numeric level for each of the eight performance categories on the rubric (see Illustration 8) in addition to their current levels of knowledge for listening and written theory skills. Once you establish the starting score for each area, then you can discuss what each student needs to do individually to make progress.

Let's begin with establishing a baseline score for the eight performance factors on the rubric. Performance assessment, which will end up being a grade at the end of the term, should be thought of as a "purpose" continuum, as shown in Illustration 13 with classroom formative and diagnostic assessments at one end and high-stakes summative assessments at the other. Informal classroom observations are to the left of the continuum: teacher's planned classroom assessment events e.g., a teacher/student music check-off of parts, or a group playing/singing together are in the center of the continuum and externally set high-stakes assessments, such as a solo or ensemble performance at contest or an end-of-the-year jury performance are to the right. Recall we had decided, based upon the research on grading, to have numerous and a variety of performance opportunities that would be used to measure the students' academic and musical growth? The picture below illustrates how a student performance assessment moves from informal to formal.

ILLUSTRATION 13

PURPOSE CONTINUUM

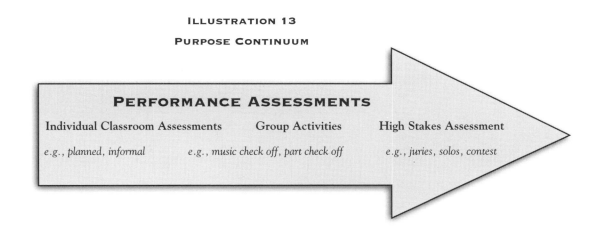

PERFORMANCE ASSESSMENTS

Individual Classroom Assessments	Group Activities	High Stakes Assessment
e.g., planned, informal	*e.g., music check off, part check off*	*e.g., juries, solos, contest*

If there is a base score at the beginning of the term for each student, similar to the one in Illustration 14, then one can compare the scores at the end of the semester or set time period. It is possible to measure the performance growth in each of the eight categories and use that data as the basis for their grade. The student can clearly see the areas of skill weakness, and thus will be able to target extra effort with the help of the teacher to make improvement in those areas while maintaining skills that are strengths.

ILLUSTRATION 14

BASELINE SCORE

Joe Smith's Performance Baseline Scores, September 2011

	Tone Quality	Intonation	Rhythm	Technique*	Interpretation, Musicianship*	Diction, Bowing, Articulation	Performance Factors	Scales
5								
4.5							▓	
4		▓					▓	
3.5	▓	▓					▓	▓
3	▓	▓	▓	▓			▓	▓
2.5	▓	▓	▓		▓	▓	▓	▓
2	▓	▓	▓	▓	▓	▓	▓	▓
1.5	▓	▓	▓	▓	▓	▓	▓	▓
1	▓	▓	▓	▓	▓	▓	▓	▓

ILLUSTRATION 15

JANUARY PERFORMANCE SCORES

Joe Smith's Performance Baseline Scores, January 2012

	Tone Quality	Intonation	Rhythm	Technique*	Interpretation, Musicianship*	Diction, Bowing, Articulation	Performance Factors	Scales
5								
4.5							▓	
4	▓						▓	
3.5	▓	▓	▓	▓			▓	▓
3	▓	▓	▓	▓	▓		▓	▓
2.5	▓	▓	▓	▓	▓	▓	▓	▓
2	▓	▓	▓	▓	▓	▓	▓	▓
1.5	▓	▓	▓	▓	▓	▓	▓	▓
1	▓	▓	▓	▓	▓	▓	▓	▓

*Indicates the skills targeted by the student during the semester.

Let's compare Joe Smith's September scores with his January scores (See Illustration 15). Tone, rhythm, and scales have all improved by .5, which in one semester is a large gain. What is more impressive, however, is that technique has increased by 1.5 and interpretation/musicianship has increased by 1.0. It is obvious that the student targeted these two areas and was able to demonstrate his ability to improve those areas through performance. He should receive a grade to reflect that skill growth. In *Scale Your Way to Music Assessment* (chapter 8, "Formulate Assessment"), we go into detail about how to teach students how to assess themselves and how the teachers have to agree on the standard for measuring students. In order to have reliable measures of musical growth, teachers must agree upon the standard that all students will be judged. In addition, the standard must be clearly articulated, both in writing and in some type of recordings, so students can hear what the numeric rating sounds like. Clarifying the standard for each level will assist student understanding so they know what they need to do to move to the next level. Now answer this question.

If a player is weak in tone, intonation, rhythm, and articulation, is it even possible to play at a high level in the Interpretation/Musicianship column?

_____

_____

In order to take a number and turn it into a grade, we had to establish just how much the average student musician would be expected to musically grow in one semester in each of the areas. For example, it was far easier for students to improve their scores in the scales column than in the interpretation/musicianship column. Scales are less demanding and are more technical and straightforward to assess; the notes are either played correctly and remain at the same tempo or not. On the other hand, interpretation and musicianship has numerous subjective aspects to it. The student needs to synthesize a variety of higher-level skills such as dynamics, emotional involvement, phrasing, style, and tempo to improve that score. This synthesis is what we want our students to ultimately strive for. Answer the following question using your current system of grading.

What grade would you give our hypothetical student, Joe Smith, in your grading system? What weight would you assign to each category?

_____

_____

_____

Here is how we weighted the scores. First, the charts in Illustrations 14 and 15 represent only one score from the three areas—performance, listening, and written theory. We valued the musical performance score more than the listening and written theory scores and weighted them accordingly. The skills each student had selected as a target on the goal sheet also had more weight. In the Joe Smith example, he chose to focus on technique and interpretation/musicianship. We found if the student, with the help of the teacher, wrote about specific skills to improve, then the student would take responsibility for doing the work to improve those skills. We wanted to have tasks that the students valued and where they had a variety of opportunities to demonstrate those skills through performance.

Our weighting would look like this for Joe Smith, the hypothetical student. With the teacher's help, each student selected different goals and areas of weakness to work on so this weighting applied specifically to this student. For Joe Smith, the targeted area of technique and interpretation/musicianship would be weighted at forty percent of the performance grade and the other six areas would each be worth ten percent for a total of 100 percent. Forty percent was arrived at because he valued the higher-level skill areas more, and these skills also happened to be the area the student had targeted that semester.

Which begs the question, how does one compare the top student's growth with the lower-level student's growth in, for example, the skill of interpretation/musicianship?

We accomplished this differentiated grading by making sure the students were performing music appropriate to their skill levels. Music and exercises were selected based upon the level of music on which the student could demonstrate the eight categories of skills. If a director has only one piece of music that everyone is going to play, regardless of the student's skill level, then it is obvious what the outcome will be. Higher-level students will perform better than lower-level students. We want all the students to demonstrate in the interpretation/musicianship skills, which is what we value? This higher-level skill must be reached regardless of what level students are at in their skill development. If one can challenge and select music that is at or slightly above the student's current skill levels, then the student will have a measure of success on that level. That feeling of success will motivate them to continue to work at raising their skill level each quarter or semester. The music they are being rated on comes in several forms: music for concerts, solos, etudes, and other skill-building exercises.

SELECTING MUSIC

It is possible to hear groups play music far past their ability level. Often directors will select music without understanding the ability of their students. Directors will select music they want to play or perhaps played in college. Over the course of the next six to eight weeks in rehearsal, they virtually beat the music out of the students, often working on notes and skills that were areas of weakness for the students and never getting to the music. Take some time to answer the questions below.

How and why did you select the music you performed on your last concert?

_____

_____

Were you correcting notes right up to the performance?

_____

_____

Are you repeating yourself in rehearsal, making the same comments about dynamics, phrasing etc.?

_____

_____

Are you frustrated at times with your students' musical growth?

_____

_____

Do you feel that each year you are repeatedly teaching the same skills and knowledge?

_____

_____

Have you ever heard outside of rehearsal each student perform individually all the music for a concert?

_____

_____

TAKING TIME TO HEAR YOUR STUDENTS INDIVIDUALLY

Let's address the question about having students perform individually for their director. When working to change the learning environment, we recorded several rehearsals and then listened to them, focusing on what we were saying from the podium. We were repeating ourselves and that the rehearsal didn't sound like a lot of fun. A realization came after talking to some students that the comments in rehearsal were said to everyone. In reality, they should have addressed a few students who were not making the corrections requested. To check this observation, every single student was asked to come in and play the music we were rehearsing. The number of small mistakes from all the students not heard from the podium was amazing. Additionally, the mistakes that were supposed to be fixed in rehearsal were still being made. Two questions came to mind after hearing all of the students play.

1. How would one ever get to the music if even a small percentage of the students didn't take responsibility for learning the music?

2. How could a conductor expect students to learn music they do not have the skills to play?

To make a long story short, I adjusted the score parts of the students who did not have the skills and required them and everyone else to have the parts checked off by me two weeks before the concert. If the student was not willing to make the commitment to learn their parts, they would not play in the concert. I called this OFF THE RISER. If the student was not willing to make the commitment to learn their parts, they would not play the concert, which resulted in an "off the riser" for the student.

If students were off the riser, they understood what parts of the music were being played inaccurately, made sure they had the time and the support to correct the music and come back and play for the conductor, a stratagem that worked. Although the off the riser students were improving their individual skills, the rest of the band was rehearsing the music. The environment of rehearsing was changed as was the student's responsibility for learning skill-level appropriate music. When students improve their skills so that they were able to play the parts, they would return to rehearsal and be given a round of applause by the other students who cared for their fellow musician. What changed? The students saw the grades they received based upon the multiple performances on the skills. They did not think of the grade as only learning the music skills needed to play the concert. They understood why they received the grade and were able to understand what had to be done to improve their skills and ultimately the grade, which gave them the skills to perform with the group.

Following are some questions for your students.

1. Is it fair for students that have no intention of developing musical skills to continue to disrupt rehearsals with mistakes they could fix?

2. Should comments from the podium be made directly to the students making the mistakes or to everyone in general, broad statements?

3. Should students who are unable to play the music be given extra help?

4. If mistakes are continually made and not corrected, do you really know who is making them?

THE POWER OF ILLUSTRATING HOW INDIVIDUALS RELATE TO THE GROUP

Now let us return to the subject of using data as information. The graph in Illustration 16 shows the entire concert band's performance scores of which our student, Joe Smith, is a member. What we want Joe to understand from this data is where his individual scores are in relationship to the entire group. Students are accustomed to seeing test scores on standardized exams and where they are in relation to the state and national scores. Since music does not have state and national scores available, it is important for Joe to see where he is musically in relation to his current performing group.

ILLUSTRATION 16

SEMESTER I CONCERT BAND OVERALL PERFORMANCE SCORE*

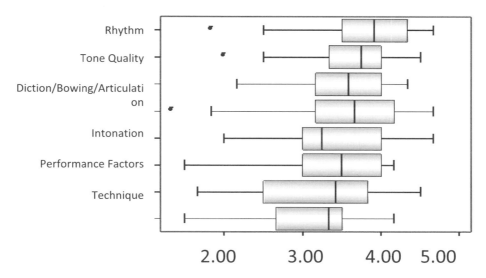

We believed this understanding was important for two reasons. First, Joe can see that although he is showing improvement each semester, he still needs to focus on his weak areas to contribute even more to the group. Second, we want Joe to celebrate his achievements in his strong areas. One score for all eight categories does not reflect his success in specific skills. But, what this conversation really does is give the teacher and the student a sense of where they are in their musical journey and what each of them needs to do to move the group ahead. The teacher sees areas in which to improve and the student understands his role in improving his efforts to help the group. The power behind the grade and the assessment data you are providing your students is remarkable. Indeed, the conductor is giving the students a snapshot of where they are in becoming an Independent Musician Creating Quality Performances. It's time for another question.

How would your concert music selection change if you had the information about student abilities both as a group and individually?

_____

_____

*A detailed explanation can be observed in the box plot (Figure 23) in *Scale Your Way to Music Assessment* (pages 68-69). Basically, a box plot is a horizontal line with vertical lines, known as whiskers, at each end and a gray box in between these lines. The box encompasses 50 percent of the ratings, from the 25th to the 75th percentile and the other 50 percent of the ratings fall outside the box. The vertical black line inside the box marks the 50th percentile, or the median. The whiskers (vertical lines at the end of the horizontal line) mark the lowest and highest ratings for each category.

Of utmost importance, this information allows the teacher to grade students accurately and encourages teachers to adjust their instruction. Improving instruction is what good teaching is all about. If we don't adjust our teaching to what the data are saying, then we are not providing the educational opportunities our students, parents, and communities expect.

GRADING LISTENING AND WRITTEN THEORY SKILLS

Let's continue to look at how we would apply the same method of grading to the other two areas we valued, listening and written theory skills. As we did with the performance skills, we would first establish the level of individual student understanding at the beginning of the year. Students who were in grades 10, 11, and 12 would use the data from the previous year's semester tests and a short test on the current year's new skills. (On pages 123 to 134 in *Scale Your Way to Music Assessment*, you will see a complete list of the skills that we valued for each year, which would be the skills on which the students would be assessed.) Freshmen did not have any data from the previous year, so we would give a series of sample questions on the material to be tested and that would be used to select weak and strong areas of focus. If you are in a K-12 system, can you imagine how powerful the learning would be if you had a system that sequenced and targeted skills and assessments in a progression from kindergarten through high school?

Of special note: Most of our freshmen had no background in hearing intervals, identifying intervals on paper, or a basic understanding of theory. We knew that most the students would be learning this material for the first time and would need to have a sliding grading score that separated those students who had no background from the ones who had previous training. A sliding scale would allow a student with no previous training who scored a 50 percent on a January final to earn an "A" since they made significant progress. Students with previous background knowledge would have a different sliding score, and they would be expected to demonstrate more growth from the pre-test to the January final. At the end of the year final in May, all freshmen students would be graded on the same scale, which allowed for students to all reach the same level but at their own pace.

After looking at the scores from the pre-test or last year's data, the students would select areas that needed work. They would write their specific goals on the goal sheet and begin working to improve those skill areas. The teacher also would have looked at the data from the last year and adjusted the teaching methods to account for less than expected growth in certain skill areas. Notice, we are talking about numbers and skills, not grades. The student received a grade last year based upon individual growth. Now we were focusing on skill building and not working for a particular grade. This information relates back to chapter 8, in which we wanted to change the learning environment to be one in which students were seeking mastery.

TRANSLATING PROGRESS INTO A GRADE

In each of the areas below, students would have received the results of all the data from each test or assessment. The scores would show how many correct responses the student received in each of the skill levels that would then be compared to the average of the performing group or class.

YEAR 1 FINAL - WRITTEN THEORY

Volume 1, Unit 1*   Staff, Notes and Pitches
Volume 1, Unit 2   Note Values, Time Signatures, and Rests
Volume 1, Unit 3   Time Signatures, Ties and Slurs
Volume 1, Unit 4   Repeats, Eighth Notes, and Dotted-Quarter Notes
Volume 1, Unit 5   Dynamics, Tempo Marks, Articulation, D.C., and, D.S.
Volume 1, Unit 6   Flats, Sharps, Naturals, Whole/Half Steps, and Enharmonics
Volume 2, Unit 7   Tetrachords, Scales, and Key Signatures
Volume 2, Unit 8   Key Signatures, Chromatics, and Intervals
Volume 2, Unit 9   Intervals, *Solfége*

*Volumes and Units refer to the theory workbook.

YEAR 1 FINAL - LISTENING

Interval Recognition-Visual (ascending only)
Correct Notation-Listening
Rhythm and Notes
Rhythm-Visual
Scale Recognition-Visual/Listening
Intervals-Not Visual
Triads-Not Visual
Intervals-Visual

The charts in Illustration 17 and 18 indicate the skills growth of a group, either performing groups or all students in a particular grade, from January to June. The data show that students' musically grew significantly in all of the skill areas. A student could compare his individual musical growth to the average musical growth of the group in the categories of listening or written theory. We could examine the data further regarding specific skills such as staff, notes, pitches, rhythms, etc., so the student could see individual skill growth and how she related to the skill growth of the group. This process was also used to inform students of their progress in the eight performance skills earlier.

ILLUSTRATION 17

IMPROVEMENT FROM JANUARY TO JUNE EFFECT SIZES BY ENSEMBLE

(AVERAGE GROWTH/SD)

	Varsity Treble	Mixed	Percussion	Concert Band	Treble	Honors Madrigal
Listening Test	1.181	0.545	0.220	0.657	0.430	0.109
Written Test	1.040	0.725	0.783	0.383	0.471	0.558

ILLUSTRATION 18

IMPROVEMENT FROM JANUARY TO JUNE EFFECT SIZES BY GRADE

(AVERAGE GROWTH/SD)

	Total	Freshman	Sophomore	Junior	Senior
Listening Test	0.546	0.694	0.721	0.232	0.443
Written Test	0.581	0.637	0.612	0.792	0.277

How would we grade the individual improvement as compared to the class improvement? Let's take an example from the Mixed Choir scores in Illustration 17. The average improvement in listening scores was 0.545 and the average written theory improvement was 0.725. The closer the score is to 1.0, the greater the improvement. Because the score represents an average, some students musically grew more and some less. We would not use the group score to give an individual student a grade. We would use the information of the group's growth, combined with the breakdown of skill scores, to adjust our teaching, not to assign a grade. If, for example, a student improved more than the average, we would look at the baseline score of the pre-test. Remember, we had some students who had no prior music training in a class with highly-trained students. If the untrained student made more than the average growth, then that was because they had few skills and lots of room to improve. The opposite is also true. The highly trained student might have little room to grow and may show a lesser amount of improvement because she is already at a high level. That is why we would use a multiplier to figure out the grade for each student.

USING SIGHT-READING AS AN APPLICATION OF HIGHER-LEVEL SKILLS

Represented in chapter 5 in Illustration 4, one can see that both director long-term goal 3 and student long-term goal 2 included improving sight-reading skills. As a department, we believed sight-reading synthesized student skills in the three areas of performance, listening, and written theory into one high-level demonstration of competence. This one short individual performance allowed us to see firsthand what a student could do with the knowledge and skills we thought we had taught. We wanted to see if we were really developing Independent Musicians Creating Quality Performances.

In rehearsal, directors often ask students to read music they have never seen before: when selecting music for the next performance. We want them to figure out the key, understand how the rhythms are counted, figure out the tempo markings, in addition to any accents or symbols in the music that communicate how the selection should be played. Sight-reading was a part of our culminating experience at the end of the semester, the Jury. Because sight-reading is done individually, we were able to see the student practice the selection for one minute. The student had to demonstrate the strategies that allowed them to play a piece from sight. They had to play the scale that matched the key, clap and count the rhythms aloud, and practice singing *solfége* or playing the piece before playing it straight through for the judges. Talk about a culminating event and the absolute indicator of an independent musician! The teachers were able to have students actually demonstrate their skills and knowledge rather than guessing about what they could do. We would score the sight-reading for two purposes. First, the teachers could see were they needed to adjust their efforts from an instructional standpoint. Second, students could receive feedback about their current level of proficiency in sight-reading.

Having students sight-read without being graded is vital. Teachers don't have to grade everything, but we should provide the student with feedback. Once again, we return to the idea that we wanted to create a climate for mastery learning in which an emphasis is on effort and development. We wanted the focus for student and teacher to see that time spent learning equaled greater understanding. So, we did not grade sight-reading; we provided the results to both teachers and students with no fear of failure on the student's part. Students often know if they did well or not. Our hope was that they would take the data from the performance and use it to adjust their efforts for their next performance.

Administrative Perspective

The trend in assessment is moving away from paper and pencil standardized tests to more authentic, performance-based experiences that allow students to demonstrate a variety of skills that will be needed in the real world. Assessments will be given more often and be individualized so that student intellectual, emotional/expressive, and musical growth can be monitored and progress evaluated.

Student intellectual and musical growth will also be a part of a teacher's evaluation. One could challenge music educators to be the deciders about how they want student academic and musical growth to factor into their evaluations. If a music program does not have a valid and reliable way of measuring student growth, then that program will be subject to whatever system those in power decide. A comprehensive system of grading will provide your students with the formative feedback that will propel their musical overall performance growth. It will also provide music teachers with the data that will allow them to be evaluated fairly and consistently on the individual and group growth of their students.

CHAPTER 10
THE ARTS CONNECTION TO THE COMMON CORE

Some assessment opportunities in the music classroom may involve skills that support the Common Core State Standards. Understanding what those standards are and how they can support learning in the music classroom is vital for music educators. Today's music and general classroom teachers need to be well-versed in developing language, literacy, and content skills in their classrooms. Providing a framework to strengthen student literacy skills while students develop or enrich their base of musical knowledge should be part of a music department's curriculum. Additionally, you will also be able to further justify the importance of music as an integral part of your school, if you can demonstrate how these standards are reinforced in the music classroom.

Following are examples of high school anchor standards for reading and writing that are specifically tied to literacy in technical subjects such as music.

Reading Standards for Literacy in Science and Technical Subjects (www. corestandards.org)

KEY IDEAS AND DETAILS

1. Cite specific textual evidence to support analysis of texts attending to the precise details of explanations or descriptions.
2. Determine central ideas or conclusions of a text; trace the text's explanation or depiction of a complex process, phenomenon, or concept; provide an accurate summary of the text.
3. Follow precisely a complex multi-step procedure.

Craft and Structure

4. Determine the meaning of symbols, key terms, and other domain-specific words and phrases.
5. Analyze the structure of the relationships among concepts in a text, including relationships among key terms.
6. Analyze the author's purpose in providing an explanation, describing a procedure, or discussing an experiment in a text, defining the question the author seeks to address.

Integration of Knowledge and Ideas

7. Translate quantitative or technical information expressed in words in a text into visual form and translate information expressed visually or mathematically into words.

8. Assess the extent to which the reasoning and evidence in a text support the author's claim or a recommendation for solving a problem.

9. Compare and contrast findings presented in a text to those from other sources, noting when the findings support or contradict previous explanations or accounts.

Range of Reading and Level of Text Complexity

10. Read and comprehend complex texts independently and proficiently

WRITING STANDARDS FOR LITERACY IN HISTORY/SOCIAL STUDIES, SCIENCE AND TECHNICAL SUBJECTS

Text Types and Purposes

1. Write arguments focused on discipline-specific content.
2. Write informative/explanatory texts.
3. Not applicable

Production and Distribution of Writing

4. Produce clear and coherent writing in which the development, organization, and style are appropriate to task, purpose and audience.

5. Develop and strengthen writing as needed by planning, revising, editing, rewriting, or trying a new approach, focusing on addressing what is most significant for a specific purpose and audience.

6. Use technology, including the internet to produce, publish, and update individual or shared writing products, taking advantage of technology's capacity to link to other information and to display information flexibly and dynamically.

Research to Build and Present Knowledge

7. Conduct short as well as sustained research projects to answer a question or solve a problem; narrow or broaden the inquiry when appropriate, synthesize multiple sources on the subject, demonstrating understanding of the subject under investigation.

8. Gather relevant information and assess the usefulness of each source; integrate the information selectively to maintain the flow of ideas, avoiding plagiarism and following a standard format for citation.

9. Draw evidence from informational texts to support analysis, reflection, and research.

Range of Writing

10. Write routinely over extended time frames (time for reflection and revision) and shorter time frame for a range of discipline-specific tasks, purposes, and audiences.

Consider how many of the assessment and learning activities in this book demand the literacy skills outlined in these standards. For example, when students write specific goals for music skills, aren't they providing an argument (Writing Standard 1) by stating a claim (the goal) and supporting it with evidence of how they are going to accomplish it? Furthermore, if you have students reflect on a performance, they will again have to state a claim or opinion about the performance (Writing Standard 1) and then produce a clear and coherent reflection in which the development, organization, and style are appropriate (Writing Standard 4). When you think about it, any type of writing done in the music classroom most likely will fit into one of these standards. And, think of how powerful it will be when you can show your administration and parents that you are addressing state and national standards in your music classroom.

If you and your school community value addressing these standards that transcend all disciplines, then you should factor these into your grading system. For example, a category for Goal/Planning/Review could reflect the quality of writing and thinking related to these standards. And, as a result, your music department would be supporting the goals of the entire school and further justify the importance of music in the curriculum.

CHAPTER 11

FREQUENTLY ASKED QUESTIONS RELATED TO GRADING

How can I motivate an unmotivated student?

Regardless of the subject matter, a certain percentage of students may be unmotivated in developing their musical skills. Students may not be motivated for a variety of reasons. It could be a defense mechanism to protect them from feeling as though they failed. This reaction may occur when students are performance oriented and their sense of self-worth is tied to a self-perception that musical talent is innate. If the performance-oriented student doesn't try, he can then blame his lack of success on not trying rather than calling attention to his lack of what he thinks is innate musical talent.

Lack of motivation may also be a call for attention or perhaps the student didn't connect to the subject or value the skills she would develop. Either way, these students are in our classrooms and often turn into what may be referred to as "energy leeches." Leeches are organisms that suck the blood from another animal. If they don't suck that blood, they die. Unmotivated students can become "rehearsal leeches." They drain energy from the group, teachers tend to focus on them, and they are often disruptive to the teaching and learning process. If teachers don't change their assessment and grading system, they will never create a satisfactory climate or culture for learning in their rehearsals. Below are suggestions for minimizing the number of unmotivated students and, by extension, retaining them in your ensembles that we initiated.

1. We created a system that overtly *showed* students the connection between what we were asking them to do and how it *applied* to their current world or the one they were going to after they graduated.
2. We did not assign meaningless assignments that students felt were unimportant.
3. We monitored student progress often and gave positive feedback to help move them ahead toward achieving their goals.
4. We had a variety of performance opportunities that were not graded to encourage effort and persistence.
5. We created small, successful experiences that would build toward a more complex culminating experience.
6. We shifted the culture of responsibility and ownership for musical growth to the student.

Directors who want peak performing groups must create a culture in which grades become second to the importance of group cohesion and growth through the improvement of individual skills.

What about that unmotivated student that doesn't seem to respond?

For the chronically unmotivated students, in private meetings, ask them to write on paper the following statement:

I want to fail and I have no intention of doing anything to not fail.

Then have the student repeat the statement back to you.

Do you know that for the few chronically unmotivated students I encountered, not a single student ever got past writing it and saying it. Once I asked them to write it and then actually say the words, the conversation would open up. The student would begin talking with me about not wanting to fail and that they really wanted to succeed. The relationship changed as the meeting continued and the student saw that I cared about her success. Together we began to figure out a way to create a path to accomplishment.

How can I prevent students from dropping music classes?

In non-required elective courses, we need to understand that students choose our classes for a reason. We must look at the reasons they drop out and not be upset or defensive about discovering that it might be something over which we have control. We surveyed every student who did not reenroll in a music class. We did it in a way so the student could see that the staff truly cared about them and that we valued their honest opinions. We found that sometimes the drop out was a flaw in our school scheduling. For example, physical education, drivers education, and health were all required in the sophomore year. The P.E. Department told students that if they did not sign up for a full year of sophomore P.E., they would return them to the freshmen program. Thus, sophomores who wanted to make room in their schedule for music, had to take the one semester of PE with freshmen—talk about putting pressure on students!

Obviously, this issue affected our sophomore enrollment in music classes. By showing the administration the results of our student surveys, we were able to change the requirements for the sophomore year. In another instance, we had a group of very bright, top of the class students provide detailed mathematical results of taking a music class that was not weighted for honors credit and how that affected their GPA. Again, having this information allowed the administration and us to "brainstorm solutions," and thus students could opt for honors credit in our upper-level performing groups.

If I change my grading system, will I lose student enrollment?

Do you remember in the statement at the beginning of the book that two members of the music department were new to the district and were trying to improve the enrollment figures in music? Our first intuition: if we did not give out A's, students would drop out. Shortly after our meeting with our principal, students began registering for classes for the next year. Remember, it was January and we were in the beginning stages of the grading journey and hadn't made any changes. We decided to ask students why they did not sign up. We wanted to increase the enrollment and determine why students did not sign up was a first step.

How would you react to finding out that your grading system was seen as punitive and not based upon what the students could actually do? Students identified three reasons for not signing up as we began our journey into changing our grading system. They didn't understand how grades based upon (1.) attendance, (2.) effort, and (3.) participation was determined and when the grades were assigned, they were inconsistently done. Hearing the students repeat this complaint repeatedly again reinforced our resolve to change our method of grading and to lower the emphasis on non-achievement areas. Our enrollment in music did not drop; in fact, we lost fewer students as a result of having a fair and consistent grading practice.

Will students behave in class or come to performance events if I don't give them points for participation?

Perhaps you are listing all the reasons why you have to grade participation. "Students won't come to our performances," or "I won't be able to get them to behave in class," or "I've always had participation as a part of my grades and it's a way to reward student effort in class."

I also think you grade participation because when you went to school, your music teachers awarded grades based upon participation, and you have never been in a program that didn't grade participation.

What if you had grown up in a system that had a culture in which students attended concerts, participated in rehearsal on a high level every day, and gave whatever amount of effort it took musically to move themselves and the group ahead each rehearsal? Have you ever been in a group where the expectations for effort, participation, and attendance were understood by everyone and it was not graded?

Here is how we changed our thinking by changing the culture of our classes and the department. First, we clearly stated what the effort, participation level, and the attendance philosophy was for our department and our performance classes. We communicated it to the students, parents, and also with the administration. If the stake holders did not understand the needs of a performance class, then we would have huge issues to address. Initially, our students and parents, reacted similarly: they had never experienced a program in which, effort, participation, and attendance were clearly stated and part of the cultural norms.

You may think, "But, we do that and students still miss performances or don't give enough effort in class." The key: change needs to be a cultural one. It won't happen overnight, but it will if you persist.

When the music faculty talked about this issue, we found we had very few students who would not attend a performance on purpose. We also realized only a fraction of students did not try their best in class each day. (remember the "energy leeches"?) So, why were we subjecting everyone to this less than productive grading system? We thought if you are having to grade on effort or participation during class, then you probably have major complications. This author works with teachers throughout the country, and if they have those issues, it doesn't take long for teachers to realize that they have created a dysfunctional system of rewards and punishment instead of keeping the focus on music. Once they realize they have created the problem, we begin to look for solutions, mainly by limiting the focus on rewards and punishments. We then consider how both teachers and students can change the culture of student expectation.

Let's go back to the idea about how teachers can control many issues in the classroom. A person can always find an excuse or someone to blame. But really, in the end, it comes down to you and you only. If you would like to e-mail me, feel free to do so at pkimpton@mpae.net and let's explore possible solutions to your school-specific problem.

What if I'm still having issues getting my students to put forth effort?

If we still think that students, in our opinion, were not giving enough effort, we would bring them in individually and discuss how they were interacting in rehearsal. Yes, we made sure the discussion was private. We would explain that students who tend not to give as much to the group usually don't prepare parts and learn the musical skills needed to become an active participant in the group. Without the proper daily energy, they probably would not internalize the music we were teaching. Additionally, we would point out that when they would come and individually play, we would be able to hear that in their playing and they would end up having to come back to be able to demonstrate that they could play the music. We would not grade the effort in class, just the end product of how they could demonstrate their skills in assigned music.

Finally, here is how we dealt with the few students who would miss a performance. We stated in a written policy that was approved by our administration and given to parents and students to read and sign. The policy read, *Attendance at performances is expected, and if you miss for any reason, you will be given new music to prepare and play for the staff in order to demonstrate the skills that would be performed at the concert.*

If a student missed a performance then he did not receive the music assessment points he earned when he played for me individually. The premise of those points was: if you can play the music, then the final part of the music performance points would give you the opportunity to demonstrate playing those selections under a different set of circumstances. That setting would include a live performance in front of an audience where you could not stop in a different setting such as an auditorium or performance hall. If you don't attend, we can't duplicate that experience, and so you will need to be evaluated on music skills that duplicate a different type of musical experience. This simulation would allow the student to learn additional musical skills. In the twelve years that we implemented that system, we have had no complaints from students or parents about them having to do something musical for a missed performance.

It should also be noted that our policy included the phrase *for any reason*. That meant the faculty was not the judge or jury in deciding if an excuse for missing a performance was legitimate. The absence was never about the reason; instead we wanted the students to be evaluated on music, not their attendance. There were three students over twelve years who did not come and get the new music and perform it. Those three students who did not make up the music performance had bigger problems than attendance, but they could not argue about the evaluation of their musical skills. We were giving them a musical and educational experience to make up for the one they had missed. The focus was on the music. The reason we had only three culprits: we had created a culture in which the students wanted to be in the group. They had done the work getting ready and not enjoying the performance was really not an option in the students' minds. We had changed the culture in which everyone wanted to be at the performance.

Is not giving zeros really fair to students who did the work?

Remember, if students missed a performance, they would learn new music to demonstrate their musical skills. We did not give the student a zero for the missed performance. We wanted to keep the focus on learning music. Our music faculty read the research about the impact of zeros and as indicated in an earlier chapter, mathematically a zero is a deep hole to get out of, which often dooms the student to failure. In music, we want the student to learn and prepare music at its highest level. That is why we had numerous chances for students to come back, if they didn't earn the musical score they wanted. We made ourselves available so students could receive additional help. We wanted them to understand that repeated demonstration of music skills should not be punished. We had no rules such as a student could only earn a percentage of the points back that he could have earned the first time. No, students had the opportunity to earn their full score, the reason: we valued having students succeed. If students want to continue to improve their skills, why would we not support that effort?

You may respond, "But, aren't you punishing the student who came in the first time and played at a high level by allowing others to come back and attain the same points? Is that fair?"

Our response is to ask you what is your definition of fair? Can you refute the idea that helping all students reach their potential is what is fair? The students who came back learned quickly that they probably could have learned the music the first time around. They often changed their ways, since it was a lot harder to make up the work rather than doing it right the first time. But, if the same students continued to return, we would then begin to use the Planning and Reflection sheet to teach them how to stop procrastinating. We would never give a zero for anything. We wanted students to know that we wanted them to succeed. Here is the phrase you have seen throughout the book.

L.U.C.K.
There is no such thing as luck—there is only Laboring Under Correct Knowledge.

People do not become competent at anything if they do not do the work.

How can conductors possibly hear all their students individually several times during a semester?

Clearly, time is limited, but, we realized that every day one has a choice about how to spend their time. As teachers, we live life in forty-five or fifty minute chunks, with five minutes for getting ready for the next chunk of time. As our department developed our assessment and grading program, we determined we couldn't create more time for rehearsals, but we could make that time more effective, if the students understood why they were there and what we expected. So, it led us to to conclude we had three types of time: time in rehearsal; time for individually working with students; and time for life outside the school.

TIME IN REHEARSAL

Once we had changed the culture and our expectations for the development of skills in music, we found we had more time in rehearsal. We had more time because we did not say or teach the same thing over and over again. In chapter 10, it is explained how we had recorded ourselves and then listened to our rehearsals using a stop watch and writing down how many times we stopped, how long we talked, how often we repeated ourselves, how many sarcastic remarks we made, how many discipline or behavior corrections we had, and finally, what amount of time was spent actually playing. I challenge you to tally your own rehearsals, or have a colleague do so, and see what you find. It is a powerful and eye-opening exercise. In every case, when a teacher said they didn't have enough time, after doing the recording analysis, the teacher realized the large amount of time that was wasted during rehearsal. *You don't have the time not to change*. Once teachers created lists of skills, developed assessments, and used that data to improve instruction, the focus of their time in rehearsal shifted. They had more time to spend on the music because everyone was working for the same musical cause. Rehearsals were no longer teacher driven, they were student driven.

TIME FOR HEARING STUDENTS INDIVIDUALLY

Few directors (if any) can hear every single mistake and evaluate individuals fairly solely from the podium. If you are out there, then I challenge you to hear your students play all their parts for you individually.

Stop assessing only from the podium. It is unfair and just an excuse for the students not to take personal responsibility for developing their skills musically. Some students figure out that you are not going to catch the fact that they can't play, so why should they learn the parts. Did you notice the use of the word "catch"? Avoiding the demonstration of ability is learned behavior, and it's a behavior we don't want to support in the music classroom. However, students can't hide, if you hear them play individually outside of class. They must take responsibility for what they are doing musically, which allows you to really hear what they can do. Try it. You may be shocked to actually find out you are not hearing all the mistakes from the podium. In addition, you may discover they are playing few dynamics and are not putting much emotional musical feeling into their notes. Once we started hearing our students individually and holding them accountable for their learning, we had more time in rehearsal to spend on the interpretation of the music.

So, how did we make the time for hearing students individually? We just made ourselves available for students to come in and play before and after school, during lunch hours or anytime they could come in. I personally gave up three days from three to nine two weeks before each performance to hear every student. You can do it anyway you want, but music teachers must hear students play individually. Other teachers have to grade papers or projects or set up labs. Teachers have to do this work outside of class. We are all busy, but if you want your rehearsals to be more effective, (and enjoyable for the students and you), you will spend the time to hear your students. You will be teaching them how to *unlearn getting caught*.

Using software programs that claim to assess student performances are often a crutch. These programs are no replacement for hearing your students individually. It is the hope we never have teachers evaluated by a computer concerning how they teach. Teachers would want that face-to-face assessments of their teaching abilities, so why would we do anything less for our students. Earlier in this book, there is a paragraph explaining how the reader can find and use grading software and again we encourage you to do so.

Time for Life Outside of School

Every profession takes a large amount of people's time, if they are going to create something extraordinary. By creating a grading and assessment program for our department, however, we began to have more quality family time, because we spent less time thinking about our programs and students. One might inquire, how can I hear my students outside of the regularly scheduled class, develop assessments and a grading system, and still have time with my family? The problem: if you don't take the time to develop these programs, then your students are not joining you in the pursuit of music. You become the sole driving force. If you are the one shepherding the program, then you start spending more time in extra rehearsals and/or sectionals trying to get the students to learn the music. The real impact of having the student take responsibility in the development of their musical skills is that they can learn the music independently. Then, when the performing group is together, you can teach for what you are really after—the music, not all the mistakes that are due to a student's lack of learning the music.

Once we developed the assessments and the grading system, we began to spend less time at home thinking about the next rehearsal. Our rehearsals were more efficient and targeted to address the specific areas of skill and musical weaknesses, and thus we did not need to have extra rehearsals. All-in-all, you will spend time developing a grading and assessment system to save time for what really matters and that is finding the balance between work and home. Get the students motivated and involved and you will work less.

CHAPTER 12
NINE STEPS TO SUCCESS

This last chapter is designed to review the previous chapters and assist you on your journey into differentiated grading as you move forward in the implementation process.

By now you know how we accomplished putting music back into our system and decisions. At this junctures, your music department is ready to begin creating your own grading/assessment program that fits the needs of your school community and your department/school philosophy. Let's get started.

1. Write the reasons for change and support your answers through research.

In order to begin your grading transformation, make sure you understand the latest research and literature about the subject of grading and assessment. Be certain you have the background for both grading and assessment. There is a list of suggested readings at the end of this book. You are urged to talk with your administration for some suggestions and discuss your intended plans. If they have a process in place based upon best practices, read about them and combine the ideas from this book into your own school's grading and assessment system. Have everyone in your staff read a different book and then share what they learned with the music faculty, highlighting the parts that may apply to your school. Don't think of the reading as work, but as a way to ignite discussions about the topics. Be clear, in your mind, however, to keep the focus on facts and not opinion. Lastly, it is vital to write down your personal reasons for making changes in your grading and assessment program and have everyone in your music department do the same. As you share your reasons, you will become united as a faculty to complete this project.

2. Forget the baggage.

"Forget the Baggage" exercises is the secret to focusing on the task of changing your department's view of grading and not letting anyone's personal baggage slow or stop the group's intended mission. Everyone must make a commitment to this philosophical and psychological transformation; if so, the work will not only be rewarding, but also, it will bring the department closer together. Being united will also show the administrators, parents, and students that the faculty is keeping *music* as the primary focus and that you are doing everything possible to create an educational, student-centered environment.

3. Involve the stake holders.

Throughout this book, the intention has been to involve your administrators, parents, and students in the process. Also, you have been given several suggested questionnaires and surveys to poll students about their views of your current grading system. Students are the consumers and your faculty needs to hear what they think. You may not like what they say, but you must value their opinions. Administration! Administration! Administration! This word appears three times for a purpose because the administration must be involved throughout the entire process. In the end, any grade dispute "ends up in their laps," and you will have their support, if they have been involved and informed of the changes you are making. They often share suggestions or ideas you may not have thought about that speak to the school-wide matter of assessment and grading. Parents also need to be informed in writing when you present your new grading system. Send home each quarterly syllabus with the student expectations and have the parent sign it, indicating they have read it. An even better idea is to have a parent/student meeting at the beginning of the year and discuss the expectations and your changes, making clear the positive effect this change will have on the learning environment and, by extension, the students. In your department, discuss the best method of communication for your type of school community. You will be surprised at how grateful the parents will be when they understand the focus of your grades is music.

4. Learn how to maximize your school's grading and assessment software potential.

Grading software for schools is changing so fast and has so many fantastic applications that you need to learn how to maximize the system you have. You can always create other types of grading evaluation methods to send home that show musical growth through graphs, etc., but having a grading program that is accessible to parents will help clearly communicate where the students are in the development of their skill levels. Grades also must be entered in a timely manner. Do not create a system that you cannot regularly update and maintain. Talk to the administrator in charge of your school's grading software and get as much training as you can. Your administration also can tell which teachers in your school may help you in learning about the software programs. Additionally, find what type of assessment software your school has so you can use that software to generate charts or graphs to illustrate students' musical and intellectual growth. If they do not have any, then use JMP—pronounced "jump" If you visit their Web site www.jmp. com, there is a trial program you can download. It is vital to have good assessment software to analyze your data accurately.

5. Generate a list of skills and align the skills.

In chapters 2 and 3 in *Scale Your Way To Music Assessment*, there is detailed information about creating a list of skills and aligning them with your curriculum. In chapter 5, of the same book, there is an explanation about how to accomplish this important step. After reading those chapters it is hoped you will create a list of music skills that you value. Be aware, however, that the list should be a music department list, not just a choir or band list. First, discuss what music skills the department values, and then add any subject-specific items after you have generated the department list. Once you have created your list, align the skills with the year's planned curriculum in which they will be taught and tested. Having decided when to *teach* the skills and when to **test** the skills allows the teacher to determine *how to teach* those skills. Your department's teaching and learning culture will begin to change as the staff openly discusses ways to best teach those skills. Having a consistent approach to teaching and learning in your department is essential so all students have the best learning experiences possible.

6. Develop a rubric that clarifies skill levels.

In chapter 5, there is a discussion of performance rubrics. If your state does not have such a rubric, go to the National Federation of High Schools (NFHS) Web site www.nfhs.org and download the NFHS Music Adjudication form for solos. Having a clear rubric will communicate to your students a unified department standard for each of the eight performance areas listed. Once you have selected the rubric, you can create written descriptions for the levels of expectation so students are able to duplicate them. Additionally, these descriptions will ensure that all faculty members consistently interpret the levels. Record various examples of what the levels are so students can hear what the written description of each level sounds like. Listening provides students with a deeper understanding of what is expected at each level. Having both written and aural examples is very important. Decide, as a faculty, about what you believe the levels are so the degree of expectation is the same for each teacher in the music department.

7. Develop grading categories to monitor growth.

The categories for grading have purposely not been listed until now. Showing them to you too soon might limit your thinking as you began and arrived at your new philosophical beliefs. Each category that we used is shown in Illustration 19. If you have a grading software program, you can create a category heading so that progress in each skill can be monitored over the course of a semester. A secondary bracket indicates the performance skill areas. You will also notice three skills: interpretation/musicianship, overall performance, and sight-reading. These are the higher-level skill activities that our department valued, and thus, gave them more weight. It is important to point out we did not assign any weights to the categories because that is a discussion that will occur in your department as you determine what you value. After looking at this list, discuss what categories your department might create. Be careful not to create too many categories, especially at the beginning of your work. Also, take into consideration that not all categories are used for every assignment or assessment and that each student will have different skill weights, depending upon where they were in their skill level development. (See Illustration 19.)

8. Create multiple performance and assessment opportunities.

Offering a variety of individual performance assessments is vital in keeping the focus on music. Having one or two individual performances will not allow you the opportunity to provide the feedback necessary for significant student growth. Moreover, it will put too much pressure on students for the few assessments you do have. Have a balance of graded and non-graded performances. Remember that everything does not have to be graded, but you should provide feedback. Numerous small performances are better than a few big ones. As a department, talk about the parameters of performances and how you would create an atmosphere of learning and feedback. The same would hold true for your other assessment activities in the areas of listening and written theory. Have a variety of performances and have them often in an environment in which students can learn and practice skills over time in a risk-free atmosphere. This advice is especially true when learning skills that take time to master such as interval recognition and sight-singing.

ILLUSTRATION 19

GRADE CATEGORIES

Tone

Intonation

Rhythm

Technique

Interpretation, Musicianship

Diction–Bowing–Articulation

Other Performance Factors

Categories

Scales

Overall Performance

Sight-Reading

Listening Skills

Written Theory Skills

Goals–Planning–Review

Non–Achievement

9. **Find the time to hear your students individually.**

The above concept is discussed throughout the book and it is important to stress it one more time. Discontinue assessing solely from the podium. Find the time in your schedule to hear your students individually. This effort will accomplish two very important results. First, students will become accountable for demonstrating the skill they have learned. They can't hide and will take responsibility for learning skills in a timely manner. Furthermore, it will help students make the connection that good musicians understand their responsibility to the group and the music. Second, as the teacher, you will have a much better understanding of what your students can really sing or play and how much they have improved. Most important: you will be able to adjust your teaching methods from the podium to address the areas of performance weakness. So, make time to hear each student perform.

CHAPTER 13
FINALE

"Those who cannot change their minds cannot change anything."
—George Bernard Shaw

It is the hope of the authors that we have changed your thoughts about grading and how it is time to put *music* back into your grades. Music educators must realize that we have gotten away from why we went into the profession in the first place, and that was for the shear love of music and making music. That love for music came from developing the performance skills necessary to play and perform at a high level. The problem: we are not giving our students a fair and equal chance to succeed. If we don't create the next generation of young musicians who will stay in our programs long enough to want to support and foster music in our society, then the future for music is dim. Grading and assessment are areas where we have fallen down because we continue to use outdated systems for evaluating young musicians.

No doubt some of the ideas advanced in this book might seem radical to some musicians, but these practices are not extreme in the rest of the educational world. Music educators may resist change, but we need to reinvent our ways of thinking, if we wish to keep current and maximize our teaching time. It is the authors' hope you will see it is possible and necessary to rethink how you assess and grade your students. The challenge for you is to take the information from this book and adapt it to your own community. If music education doesn't evolve, it will die, and therefore the first step is to reexamine your assessment and grading practices.

Congratulations to you for considering embracing what we have presented here, and begin using the ideas to create your own grading system that will create Independent Musicians Creating Quality Performances. We commend you for creating the young people who are our future supporters and consumers of a very precious art form: they are our *musical legacy* for the future.

If you ever have any questions, go to our Web site www.mpae.net or www. adventureswithmusic.com_and use our message board. Send us an e-mail and/or give us a call during the times listed. We want to hear about your journey and continue to help you create a music program full of Independent Musicians Creating Quality Performances.

REFERENCES AND RESOURCES

Deci, Edward L. and Richard Flaste. (1996). *Why We Do What We Do: Understanding Self-Motivation*.

Guskey, Thomas R. (2008). *Practical Solutions for Serious Problems in Standards-Based Grading*. Thousand Oaks, CA: Corwin Press.

Robert Linn, Robert and David Miller. (2004). *Measurement & Assessment in Teaching*. Upper Saddle River, NJ: Prentice Hall.

Maehr, Martin and Larry Brakamp. (1986). *The Motivation Factor: A Theory of Personal Investment*. NY, NY: Lexington Books.

Marzano, Robert. (2000). *Transforming Classroom Grading*. Alexandria, VA: ASCD.

Marzano, Robert. (2006). *Classroom Assessment and Grading That Works*. Alexandria, VA: ASCD.

O'Connor, Ken. (2009). *How To Grade for Learning: Linking Grades to Standards*. Thousand Oaks, CA: Corwin Press.

Popham, James. (2010). *Classroom Assessment: What Teachers Need to Know*. Upper Saddle River, NJ: Pearson.

Stiggins, Richard J. (2000). *Student-Involved Classroom Assessment*. Upper Saddle River, NJ: Prentice Hall.

Stiggins, Richard J., Judy A. Arter, Jan Chappuis, and Stephen Chappuis. (2009). *Classroom Assessment for Student Learning: Doing it Right—Using it Well*. Portland, OR: ETS.

Tomlinson, Carol. (2008). *The Differentiated School: Making Revolutionary Changes in Teaching and Learning*. Alexandria, VA: ASCD.

Wormeli, Rick. (2006). *Fair Isn't Always Equal: Assessing and Grading in the Differentiated Classroom*. Portland, ME: Stenhouse Publishers.

About the Authors

Ann Kaczkowski Kimpton is an assistant principal for curriculum and instruction and former literacy department chair and teacher at a suburban Chicago high school. Mrs. Kimpton received her bachelors in English and journalism from the University of Illinois, a master's degree in reading and an Administrator's Certificate from Northern Illinois University, and has completed the coursework in curriculum and instruction for a doctoral degree. She has given numerous presentations and workshops at the local, state, and national level, and is in constant demand as an expert in literacy.

An accomplished musician, Mrs. Kimpton played French horn in the University of Illinois Symphonic Bands under the direction of Dr. Harry Begian, and she is a color guard specialist for marching bands. You might also recognize her as the mother in the Yamaha Music band recruitment video, *The Great Beginning*.

A music educator for thirty-three years, **Paul Kimpton** recently retired from his position as director of bands and department chairman at a suburban Chicago high school, where the music program was known for its innovation and high performance standards. Mr. Kimpton received his bachelors and masters in music education from the University of Illinois, an Administrator's Certificate from Western Illinois University and a Guidance/Counseling Certificate from Northern Illinois University.

Kimpton is the co-author of a best-selling music assessment book, *Scale Your Way to Music Assessment*. Along with his wife, Ann, he is the author of the *Adventures in Music Series* books, *Starting Early*, *Dog Tags*, and *Summer of Firsts* published by GIA. Additionally, Paul Kimpton has written articles for *The Instrumentalist*, the *Illinois Music Educator* magazine and is on the advisory board for the Illinois High School Association. He is a valued clinician on music assessment and grading throughout the United States and Canada. In January 2009, he was honored with the Outstanding Music Educator Award from the National Federation of High Schools.

The Podium Series
Changing Music Education One Book at a Time

Scale Your Way to Music Assessment
Grading for Musical Excellence: Putting Music Back Into Your Grades

<u>*Coming Soon*</u>
Teaching Literacy from the Podium
Stepping off the Podium

Additional Books by the Authors Available through <u>giamusic.net</u>

Also Available in the Adventures with Music Series

Book #1 – Starting Early: A Boy and His Bugle in America During WWII
Curriculum Guide to Starting Early
Book #2 – Dog Tags: A Young Musician's Sacrifice During WWII
Curriculum Guide to Dog Tags
Book #3 – Summer of Firsts: WW II is ending, but the music adventures are just beginning.
Curriculum Guide to A Summer of Firsts
For more information or to contact the authors visit <u>www.adventureswithmusic.net</u>

Coming Soon

Book 4: Stepping Up